Arensky

SIX CHILDREN'S PIECES

1. Fairy Tale

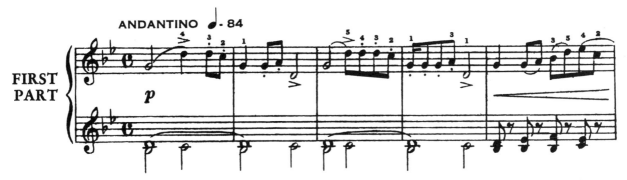

Stravinsky

Three Easy Pieces

1. March

Arensky

SIX CHILDREN'S PIECES

1. Fairy Tale

ANDANTINO ♩. 84

ANTON ARENSKY
(1861-1906)

SECOND PART

p

4 TAPS PRECEDE MUSIC

dim.

pp *p*

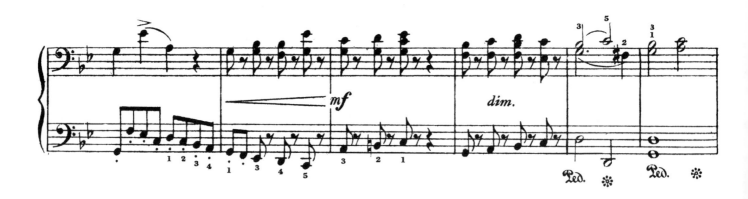

mf

dim.

Ped. ✳ Ped. ✳

pp

ppp

MMO CD 3028

1. Fairy Tale

4

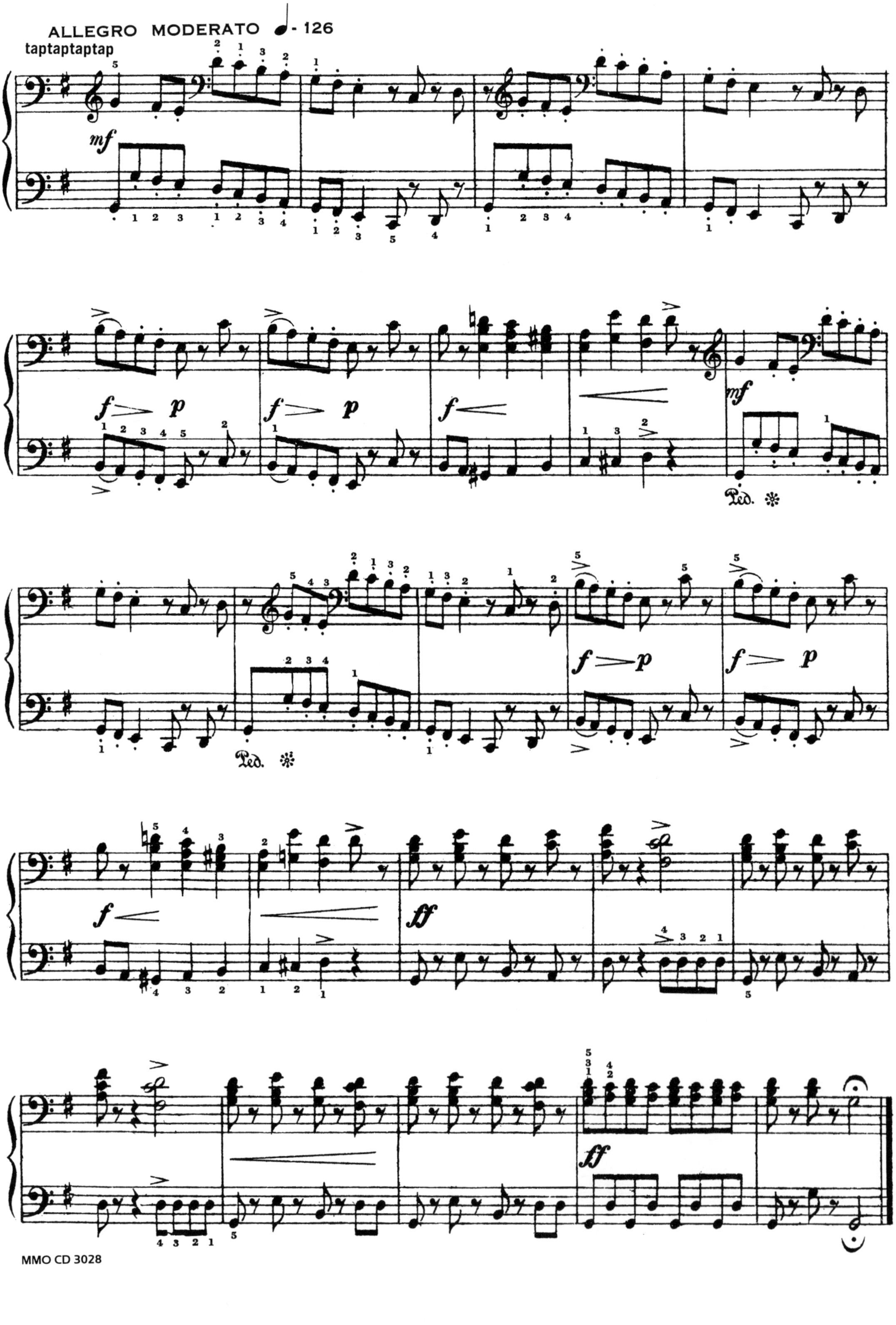
ALLEGRO MODERATO ♩- 126
taptaptaptap
mf
f
p
Ped.
ff

7

ALLEGRO MODERATO ♩= 126

taptaptaptap

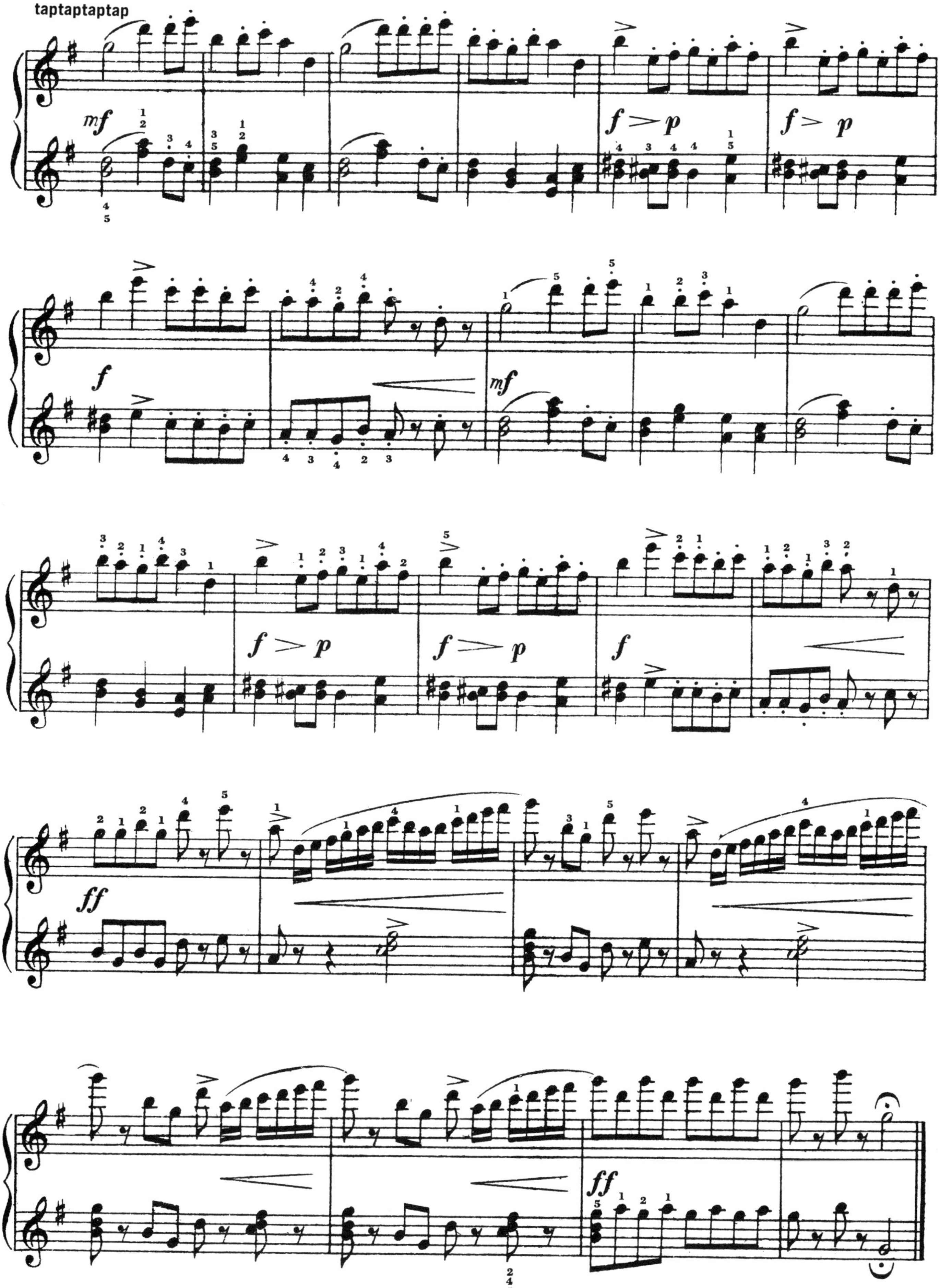

8

2. Cuckoo

2. Cuckoo

3. Tears

3. Tears

4. Waltz

4. Waltz

TRIO

TRIO

24

5. Cradle Song

5. Cradle Song

26

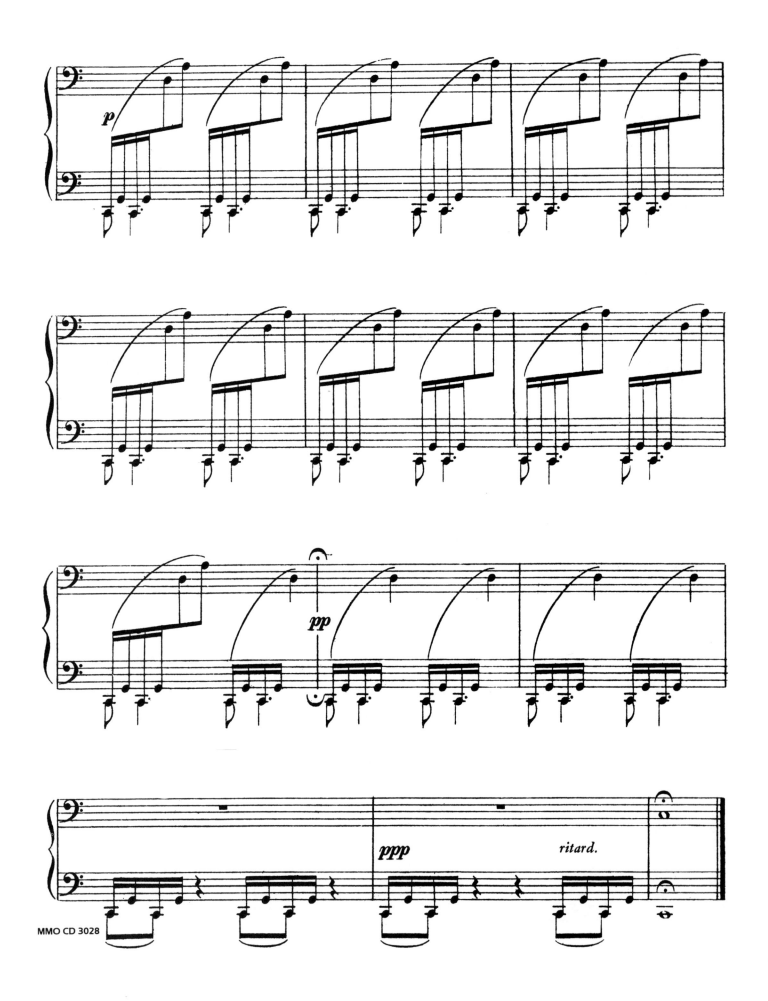

6. Fugue on a Russian Theme

6. Fugue on a Russian Theme

Stravinsky

1. March
Three Easy Pieces

SECOND PART

staccato throughout

Three Easy Pieces

1. March

FIRST PART

40

2. Valse

SECOND PART

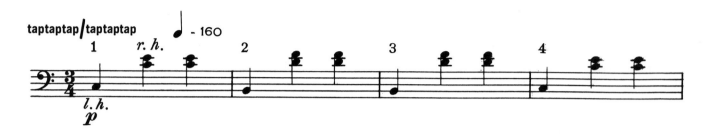

Fine

2. Valse

FIRST PART

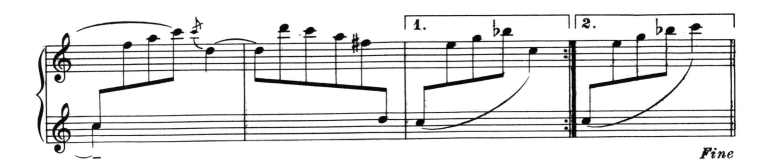

Fine

MMO CD 3028

42

D.C. al fine

Trio

poco rubato

listen to the melody

accel.

D. C. al fine

Trio

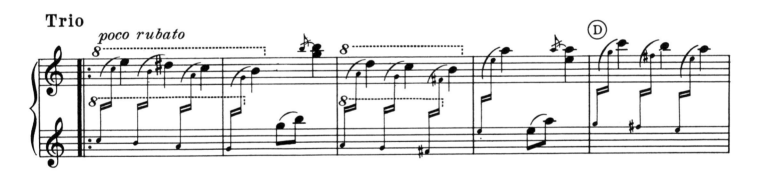

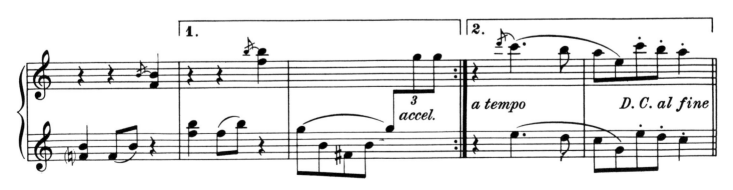

44

3. Polka

SECOND PART

MMO CD 3028

3. Polka

FIRST PART

COMPACT DISC PAGE AND BAND INFORMATION

MMO CD 3028

Music Minus One

ARENSKY

Six Piano Pieces For Four Hands

STRAVINSKY

Three Easy Pieces

MUSIC MINUS ONE

1997

Catalogue
COMPACT DISCS and CASSETTES

Participation Records for all musicians and vocalists. The most unique albums in the world.

MUSIC MINUS ONE

provides your own orchestra!

Helping students and professionals realize their musical dreams…

Welcome

to **Music Minus One** compact discs and cassettes. Since 1950, **Music Minus One** has provided the professional and amateur musician with the finest, most extensive library of play-along and sing-along recordings in the world. Our catalog of over 300 compact discs and 700 cassette editions contains some of the world's best and most requested musical literature.

In introducing compact discs into the **Music Minus One** product line, we added a professional soloist on the right channel for your reference. This valuable feature will familiarize the student with the composition and its performance. We also include the stereo orchestral background, minus the lead instrument or voice. A printed part is included with the recording. Professionals and students are now able to practice with an orchestra right in their own home. *What a great way to learn!*

We are constantly in the process of recording works that you have requested through the years. Take a look at some of the great new recordings and instruction methods available.

For those interested in popular music, we suggest you write for the free **Pocket Songs** catalog of over 10,000 songs, from nine decades of American Music. These also include 25 albums of Latin Favorites.

> *"When I was in high school, 21 years ago, MMO helped me to master my instrument.*
>
> *Later in the Coast Guard, my proficiency on the trombone and the unique support of MMO, got me some excellent assignments in bands and as a bandmaster.*
>
> *Now after many years, I'm back to my horn and MMO will be there for me again.*
>
> *Wish me luck!"*
>
> Ken Armstrong
> Kailua, Hawaii

Music Minus One is a family owned company. It has been operated continuously by the original owners since 1950. Musicians worldwide have been helped by this unique concept. which has achieved international renown.

MUSIC MINUS ONE
50 Executive Boulevard
Elmsford, NY 10524-1325

Contents

Instrumental

Vocal

Instructional Methods

Piano

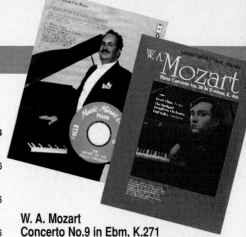

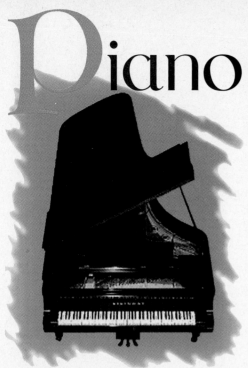

Beethoven Concerto No.1 in C, Opus 15
MMO CD 3001/314

Beethoven Concerto No. 2 in Bb, Opus 19
MMO CD 3002/316

Beethoven Concerto No.3 in C minor, Op.37
MMO CD 3003/315

Beethoven Concerto No.4 in G, Opus 58
MMO CD 3004/336

Beethoven Concerto No.5 in Eb, Opus 73
(2 CD Set)   MMO CD 3005/334

The five great piano concerti! In these works, Beethoven enlarged and intensified the breadth and scope of the classical form. Between the first and fifth piano concerto, the development of his style and his particular innovations are evident. The spirited, graceful, wonderfully pianistic Concerto No. 1 in C, written actually after the second concerto, the Mozartian Concerto No. 2 in Bb major, and the Concerto No. 3 in C minor with its striking passages, were written for and performed on a forerunner of the modern piano, lighter in tone and restricted in dynamic range. The introspective yet lofty Concerto No. 4 in G major, not popular until Mendelssohn revived it in 1836, 30 years after it was composed, and the mighty ever-popular Concerto No. 5 in Eb major, named "Emperor" by an unidentified publisher, had the advantage of the more modern piano.

Grieg Concerto in A minor MMO CD 3006/312

One of the most popular offerings in the MMO catalogue. It is less demanding and moreaccessible to the serious student.

Rachmaninoff Concerto No. 2 in C minor
MMO CD 3007/333

Equally renowned as composer and pianist, Rachmaninoff dazzled the world with his piano concerto in C minor. It is immensely popular to this day. Brilliant and powerful with the beautiful lyric theme that became the popular song Full Moon and Empty Arms, it is here presented in a lovely recording, sans your part, the solo piano.

Schumann Concerto in A minor, Op. 54
MMO CD 3008/326

A favorite in piano literature, the concerto embodies the melodic grace and fine tonal textures so characteristic of the composer.

Brahms Concerto No.1 in D minor, Op.15
(2 CD Set)   MMO CD 3009/344

Chopin Concerto No.1 in E minor, Opus 11
MMO CD 3010/343

This romantic concerto is one of the composer's few works with orchestra and displays great lyricism and grandeur.

Mendelssohn Concerto No.1 in G minor,
Opus 25   MMO CD 3011/324

W. A. Mozart
Concerto No.9 in Ebm, K.271
MMO CD 3012/328

W. A. Mozart Concerto No.12 in A, K.414
MMO CD 3013/351

W. A. Mozart Concerto No.20 in D minor,
K.466   MMO CD 3014/308

W. A. Mozart Concerto No.23 in A, K.488
MMO CD 3015/323

W. A. Mozart Concerto No.24 in C minor,
K.491   MMO CD 3016/335

W. A. Mozart Concerto No. 26 in D,
K.537, "Coronation" MMO CD 3017/309

W. A. Mozart Concerto No.17 in G, K.453
MMO CD 3018/352

Liszt Concerto No.1/ Weber Concertstücke
MMO CD 3019/303

Liszt Concerto No. 2 in A/Hungarian Fantasia
MMO CD 3020/345

The Hungarian Fantasia, with its triumphal themes, sparkling cadenzas, and breathtaking finale is a gem.

J.S. Bach Concerto in F Minor
J.C. Bach Concerto in Eb   MMO CD 3021/346

Student concerti for the beginner, by father and son. J.C. Bach, the youngest son of J.S. Bach, was also a skillful and prolific composer, as this work will testify.

J.S. Bach Concerto in D Minor
MMO CD 3022/317

Haydn Concerto in D major
MMO CD 3023/311

A student level concerto, one of the most popular in the MMO Catalog.

Heart of the Piano Concerto
MMO CD 3024/341

Great themes from the most famous piano concertos. Fun for all pianists!

Bach: Brandenberg No.5 (Allegro); Concerto In D minor (Adagio) (Allegro Moderato) **C.P.E. Bach:** (Allegro Assai); **Haydn:** Concerto In D (Vivace, Allegro Assai) **Mozart:** Concerto In Eb K271 (Allegro) Concerto In D Minor K466 (Romance) (Allegro); K488 (Allegro) (Allegro Assai); K491(Larghetto); K537 (Allegro) **Beethoven:** Concerto No.1. (Largo); No.2 (Allegro Con Brio) (Adagio); Op.37 (Allegro con Brio); Op. 58 (Allegro Moderato); Op.73 (Adagio un poco moto) (Rondo-Allegro) **Mendelssohn;** Concerto No.1 In G minor (Molto Allegro) (Andante); **Schumann:** Concerto In A minor (Allegro Affettuoso) **Liszt:** Concerto No.1 (Allegro Maestoso) **Tchaikovsky:** Concerto No.1 (Allegro Non Troppo), (Andantino) **Rachmaninoff:** Concerto No.2 (Moderato) **Grieg:** (Adagio) Excerpts from the movements indicated are played.

Small numbers on far right indicate the cassette edition of each album

"Your wonderful recording is providing me with many happy hours of extra practice."

Arthur W.
Palm Bay, Florida

Themes From Great Piano Concerti
MMO CD 3025/342

More great melodies from the masters!

Bach: Concerto in D minor (Allegro Risoluto) **Haydn:** Concerto in D Major (Un Poco Adagio)(Allegro Assai) **Mozart:** Concerto in Eb K271 (Menuetto); Concerto in D K537 (Larghetto); Concerto in A K488 (Allegro) (Adagio); Concerto in D Minor K466 (Rondo-Presto); Concerto in C minor K491(Allegro) (Allegretto) **Beethoven:** Concerto No.1 in C Minor Op.15 (Allegro con Brio) (Rondo Allegro); Concerto No.5 in Eb Major Op. 73 (Allegro); Concerto No. 2 in Bb Major Op. 19 (Rondo-Molto); Concerto No.3 in C Major Op. 73 (Largo); Concerto No.4 in G Major Op. 58

(Rondo-Viv) **C.P.E. Bach:** Concerto in A Minor (Allegro Assai); **Schumann:** Concerto in A Minor (Intermezzo) (Allegro Vivace); **Mendelssohn:** Concerto No.1 in G minor (Presto) **Liszt:** Concerto No.1 In Eb Major (Allegro Animato) **Franck:** Symphonic Variations **Tschaikovsky:** Concerto No.1 in Bb minor (Allegro) (Molto Meno Mosso) **Grieg:** Concerto in A Minor Op.16 (Allegro) (Piu Lento) (Allegro Moderato) **Rachmaninoff:** Concerto No.2 in C minor (Maestoso)

Tschaikovsky Piano Concerto No.1 in Bb minor, Opus 23
MMO CD 3026/300

One of the world's most played and revered concertos. Should be in every pianists repertoire.

> *"I am enjoying my last order. I think for once in my life, I got more than I expected!!!"*
>
> Sandye S
> Richmond, Indiana

Music for Piano Four Hands

A superb series of recordings devoted to Piano Four Hands enabling the pianist to hear both parts in definitive performances by the noted artists Sondra Bianca and Harriet Wingreen. Listen to the complete performances, then perform them yourself, playing either the first or second piano part, accompanied by these artists. An ideal series for the beginner as well as for the more advanced student.

Rachmaninoff: Six Scenes 5-6th yr.   **MMO CD 3027/405**
These sonorously advanced works were written in 1894 at the age of 21.

Arensky: 6 Pieces Stravinsky: 3 Dances 2-3rd yr. **MMO CD 3028/406**
Sondra Bianca performs fugues, marches and waltzes by these masters. Simple and unique compositions worthy of the attention of pianists everywhere.

Fauré: Dolly Suite 3-4th yr.   **MMO CD 3029/407**
This teacher of Ravel, Fauré wrote this series of pieces as a dedication to his wife. It became a favorite of the four-hand genre in family music rooms worldwide.

Debussy: Petite Suite 3-4th yr.   **MMO CD 3030/408**
Composed in 1889, these pieces bear the unmistakable and inimitable style of Debussy, the quintessential Impressionist.

Schumann: Pictures from the East (Six Impromptus Op.6)
Children's Ball (6 Dance Pieces, Op.130) 4-5th yr.   **MMO CD 3031/413**
The "Pictures" were inspired by Ruckert's poem "Makamen." They are presented here along with six humorously merry dances.

Beethoven: Three Marches 4-5th yr.   **MMO CD 3032/414**
Opus 45 in C, Eb and D major, all written in1802. Some complexity but well worth the effort to master. Rewarding!

Mozart: Complete Music for Piano 4 Hands
(2CD Set) 5-6th yr.   **MMO CD 3036/402**
Here is Mozart's complete catalogue of selections for Piano 4-Hands. (Sonata In D, Bb, F, C (K.381, 358, 497, 521, Fugue In Gm, K.401 Fantasia No. 1 In Fm K.594; No. 2 In Fm K.608; Variations In G, K.501)

Maykapar: First Steps, Op.29 1-2nd yr.   **MMO CD 3041/409**
Although easy to play, these works are skillfully written and will return many hours of pleasure at the keyboard.

Tschaikovsky: 50 Russian Folk Songs 1-2nd yr.   **MMO CD 3042/401**
Traditional folklore pieces as well as original works. This album is a treasure trove of rich keyboard excellence. Sure to be a student favorite.

Bizet: 12 Children's Games 5-6th yr.   **MMO CD 3043/404**
Here's a challenging collection for the advanced and serious student.

Gretchaninoff: On the Green Meadow,
Op.99 2-3rd yr.   **MMO CD 3044/410**
Ten beautiful duet studies inspired by nature. Level as indicated. Highly accessible.

Pozzoli: Smiles Of Childhood 2-3rd yr.   **MMO CD 3045/421**
20 compositions or "Little Pieces" on Five Notes. Another excellent program for the slightly more advanced student of the keyboard.

Diabelli: Pleasures of Youth 3-4th yr.   **MMO CD 3046/420**

Schubert: Fantasia & Grand Sonata   **MMO CD 3047/403**

Popular Music

The Art of Popular Piano Playing Vol.1
MMOCD 3033/4016

A guide to contemporary styles and techniques for any level of popular piano study. Read-along and play-along with your personal piano instructor, Vinson Hill. Discover the joy of learning how to arrange and perform old favorites and current songs in the modern idiom.
Introduction; Major Scales; Intervals; What Is This Thing Called Love; Triads & Chords; Symbols; Three To Get Ready; Chord Rhythms; Arpeggios
Vinson Hill Method

Art Of Popular Piano Playing, Vol. 2
(2 cd Set) **MMO CD 3034/4019**

A sequel to volume 1, above. Contains the study of 7th chords, triads and 7th chord inversions. Such style techniques as interval waltz bass, swing bass and arpeggio bass are examined.
Learn to play: Birth of the Blues; Autumn Leaves; Chim Chim Cheree Someone To Watch Over Me; Tea For Two; Moon River; I Will Wait For You
Vinson Hill Method

Pop Piano For Starters   MMO CD 3035/1063

Easy, swinging arrangements for listening and playing along. Vinson Hill famous jazz pianist and teacher, shows you how it sounds. Then add your solo piano to the all-star rhythm section. Ideal for 2nd and 3rd year students. Eleven Standards + *YOU* and the Vinson Hill Quartet!
Hello Dolly; This Guys in Love With You; Moon River; More; The Girl from Ipanema; What the World Needs Now; I Left My Heart in San Francisco; Sunny; Alfie; Chim Chim Cheree; Love is Blue
Vinson Hill Method

Blues Piano Fusion
MMO CD 3049/4089

Eight original blues compositions covering a broad range of styles from boogie woogie to gospel to modern funk, arranged for piano, bass, drums and sax. Listen, then play along. Includes complete arrangements, suggested solo lines and performance hints for mastering blues piano styles.
Tricky Dicky; When the Spirit; Cocaine Stomp; Wailer Blues; Boogie Breakdown; Tremblin'; Yancey's Fancy; Mad Dog Blues

20 Dixieland Classics   MMO CD 3051/4024
Maple Leaf Rag; San; Sugar Foot Stomp; Copenhagen; Tin Roof Blues; Farewell Blues; Weary Blues; Why Don't You do Right?; Milenberg Joys; King Porter Stomp; Bugle Call Rag; Wolverine Blues; A Good Man is Hard to Find; After You've Gone; Basin Street Blues; Your Feet's Too Big; The Saints; Floatin' Down to Cotton Town; Do You Know What it Means to Miss New Orleans; Dallas Blues

20 Rhythm Backgrounds to Standards
MMO CD 3052/4029
Tenderly; Basin St. Blues; It's Been a Long, Long Time; Rosetta; Sentimental Journey; After You've Gone; S'posin'; When You're Smiling; Nobody's Sweetheart; Strip Poker; Make Love to Me; Drifting and Dreaming; Enjoy Yourself; Sweetheart of Sigma Chi; Angry; One for My Baby; Dinah; Mister Sandman; There will Never Be Another You; I've Heard that Song Before

From Dixie to Swing   MMO CD 3053/4094
Standards from the Dixie and Swing eras, performed by six classic players assembled for this recording by arranger pianist Dick Wellstood; "Doc" Cheatham, trumpet; Vic Dickenson, trombone; Kenny Davern, clarinet and soprano sax; George Duvivier, bass and Gus Johnson, Jr., drums.
Way Down Yonder in New Orleans; Sunny Side of the Street; Second Hand Rose; Exactly Like You; Rose of Washington Square; I Want a Little Girl; Red Sails in the Sunset; The Royal Garden Blues

Great tunes, great players, great fun!

Chamber Music

Dvorak "Dumky" Trio, Op.90 MMO CD 3037/63
Dvorak Quintet in A, Op.81   MMO CD 3038/44
Mendelssohn Trio, Op.49   MMO CD 3039/51
Mendelssohn Trio, Op.66   MMO CD 3040/51
Bolling: Suite For Flute & Jazz Piano Trio
MMO CD 3050
Baroque and Blue; Sentimentale; Javanaise; Fugace; Irlandaise; Versatile; Véloce

This Suite when first introduced, was performed by Claude Bolling and Jean Pierre Rampal. It swiftly became the most successful Chamber Music recording in history with over one-half million copies purchased. We are delighted to make it available to the pianists and flutists in our MMO family of musicians.
Claude Bolling, himself, has endorsed this recording

Bassoon

Solos for the Bassoon   MMO CD 4601
A collection of bassoon favorites, performed by Janet Grice and then by you. Excellent practice material. Your accompanist, Harriet Wingreen, NY Philharmonic Pianist.
Bach: Bouree 1 & 2 from Third Cello Suite; It is Finished from St. John Passion **Dukas:** The Sorcerer's Apprentice **Stravinsky:** Berceuse from the Firebird **Bizet:** Entr'acte from Carmen **Beethoven:** Adagio from Sextet, Op. 71 **Donizetti:** Romanza from L'elisir d'amore **Mussorgsky:** Pictures at an Exhibition (four excerpts) **Tschaikovsky:** Second Movement from Symphony No.4 in F minor, Op. 36; Third Movement from Symphony No.5 in E minor, Op. 64 **Grice:** Gone But Not Forgotten; Improvisations

Masterpieces for Woodwind Quintets
MMO CD 4602
Beethoven: Quintet, Op. 71 **Colomer:** Bouree **Haydn:** Minuet & Presto **Lefebvre:** Finale, Suite Op.5 **Mozart:** German Dance **Barthe:** Passacaille **Haydn:** Divertimento **Lefebvre:** Suite for Winds **Reid:** Woodwind Suite in Eb

The Joy of Woodwind Quintets
MMO CD 4603
Haydn: Introduction & Allegro **Mozart:** Menuet, K 421 **Deslandres:** Allegro **Danzi:** Quintet in G minor, Op. 56 #2 **Colomer:** Menuet **Bach:** Andante in Dulci Jubilo **Koepke:** Rustic Holiday **Mozart:** Andante & Contradanse K 213; Andante Grazioso (Qt. Op. 79); Allegro Molto, K 270 **Balay:** Petite Suite

ello

Dvorak: Cello Concerto in B minor Opus 104
(2 CD Set)   MMO CD 3701/353

This concerto, well-known in the cellist's repertoire, received a fine tribute from Brahms, who upon reading the score exclaimed: "Why on earth didn't I know that one could write a cello concerto like this! If I had known, I would have written one long ago!" The concerto is bright with strong melodies and rich orchestration. Its performance is a formidable undertaking for any cellist, so be warned.

The Stuttgart Symphony Emil Kahn, Conductor;
Dorothy Lawson, Cello

C.P.E. Bach: Cello Concerto in A Minor
                                  MMO CD 3702/5019

An expressive, intense work, favored by many cellists in concert.

Boccherini: Cello Concerto in Bb Major
Bruch: Kol Nidrei   MMO CD 3703/5020

The Boccherini Concerto, warm and rich in melody and nicely detailed, is frequently heard in concert halls. It is our most popular offering on the instrument to date.

The Kol Nidrei, based on the chant sung in the synagogue at Yom Kippur, when the worshipper annuls all vows made the previous year, is inspiring in its beautiful religious feeling.

Ten Concert Pieces for Cello and Piano
                                  MMO CD 3704

J.S. Bach: Adagio (Toccato in C) **Granados:** Orientale (Spanish Dance) **Ernst Bloch:** Prayer **Carl Davidoff:** At the Fountain **Mendelssohn:** Song Without Words **Faure:** Aprés Un Reve **Ravel:** Piece en Forma de Habanera **Schumann:** Fantasy Piece **Saint Saens:** Appassionato; The Swan

Schumann Concerto in A minor, Op.129
                                  MMO CD 3705/304

Claude Bolling Suite for Cello & Jazz Trio
                                  MMO CD 3706

Claude Bolling has written some of the most popular suites for instruments and jazz piano trios in the 20th century. His flute suite is considered the most popular piece of Chamber Music of the past 20 years. This recording of the Cello suite is a typical example of his music and will both thrill and challenge any cellist. This MMO recording was endorsed by Mr. Bolling

> **"I have been using the Music Minus One Dictation and Sightsinging Series since my early teen years. The series greatly enhanced my musical development and I highly recommend its use for all serious music students."**
>
> William Fielder, Dept. of Music
> Mason Gross School of the Arts

Instructional

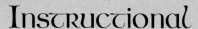

Rutgers University Music Dictation Series
(7 CD Set)   MMO CD 7001

A course in basic musicianship, ear-training and sight reading. Over seven hours of intensive study covering all of the fundamentals of music. Paced for easy learning with test materials enclosed. This series is designed for use in home or school. It is ideal for musicians and singers. Invaluable for chorus. Also available as five cassettes.

"...a listener acquainted with only the barest rudiments of staff notation could, by conscientiously working his way through the Rutgers Set acquire a respectable foundation of basic knowledge. Solid, usable matter, neither watered down, nor popularized "

John Briggs, THE NEW YORK TIMES

The Rutgers Set is now in use in over 3,000 Universities as well as in countless High Schools and by individuals around the world.

List price $98.50 per set.   7 CDs in Deluxe Album

Evolution of the Blues
Clark Terry/Bob Wilber   MMO CD 7004/1008

Blues in all styles and time signatures. Listen to the melody line then improvisation followed by jamming space for you. Indispensable!

The Art of Improvisation Volume 1   MMO CD 7005/601

Rich Matteson and Jack Petersen's course on jazz improvisation. Developed at N. Texas State Univ., the seed-bed for the stage band movement in America. C, Bb, Eb, Bass Clef parts supplied.

The Art of Improvisation Volume 2   MMO CD 7006/602

The Blues Minus You for all instrumentalists   MMO CD 7007/1011

Mal Waldron's classic study of various blues stylings, performed by Ed Xiques multi-instrumentalist, and by **you.**

Take a Chorus   MMO CD 7006/602

Stan Getz and Jimmy Raney with Ed Xiques as soloist. Join this all-star combo in standards and originals arranged by extraordinary jazz writer/player Raney.

Violin

Bruch Violin Concerto in G Minor
MMO CD 3100/330

Among the five most popular violin concerti.

Mendelssohn Violin Concerto in E Minor
MMO CD 3101/305

Mendelssohn worked on this concerto for six years. It is truly one of the most beautiful and popular in concerto literature - eloquent, passionate, lofty, brilliant.

Tchaikovsky Violin Concerto in D, Opus 35
MMO CD 3102/348

His only concerto for the violin.
A consistent favorite.

J.S. Bach Double Concerto in D minor
MMO CD 3103/307

A favorite of audiences and performers, this concerto glows with exuberance and solid structural beauty. You play either first part or second part.

J.S. Bach Violin Concerti in A Minor & E
MMO CD 3104/310

These are the two concerti for solo violin that have survived in this form. The adagio of the E major concerto is superb in its exquisite simplicity and emotion.

J.S. Bach Brandenburg Concerti
Nos. 4 and 5   MMO CD 3105/139

The amazing creativity and richness of instrumentation in these concerti have kept them to this day a most valued contribution to concert programs.

The fourth concerto, scored for two flutes, violin and string orchestra, is essentially a concerto for solo violin. The instrumentation of the fifth concerto calls for virtuoso parts for harpsichord, violin and flute.

J.S. Bach Brandenburg No. 2
Triple Concerto   MMO CD 3106/358

J.S. Bach Concerto in D minor
MMO CD 3107/319

Arranged by the composer as a concerto for clavier and orchestra.

Brahms Violin Concerto in D, Opus 77
MMO CD 3108/340

Chausson Poeme/Schubert Rondo
MMO CD 3109/354

Lalo Symphonie Espagnole   MMO CD 3110/355

Mozart Concerto in D/
Vivaldi Concerto in Am   MMO CD 3111/313

The Mozart Concerto, composed in 1775, when Mozart was 19, has an abundance of lovely melodies, and great refinement of form. Vivaldi's vibrant, firmly constructed concerti enjoyed great respect throughout Europe — his writing for the violin was widely studied and imitated.

Mozart Concerto in A, K.219
MMO CD 3112/322

Wieniawski Concerto in D Minor/Sarasate: Zigeunerweisen
MMO CD 3113/349

Viotti Concerto No. 22   MMO CD 3114/339

Beethoven Two Romances/
"Spring" Sonata   MMO CD 3115/318

The beauty and sweep of these works have made the Romances for Violin and Orchestra favorites in the artist's repertoire. Composed in 1802 and 1803, they are lyrical in style.

Saint - Saens Intro & Rondo/Mozart
Serenade No.5 K204   MMO CD 3116/329

Beethoven Concerto in D, Op. 61
(2 CD Set)   MMO CD 3117/321

Beethoven composed this work, his only violin concerto, in 1806, in the same year that he composed the Symphony No .5, the Rasoumowsky Quartets, and the piano Concerto No. 4. It was dedicated to Franz Clement, who at its premiere separated the first movement from the second and third movements and fiddled some of his own works in between, with the violin turned upside-down! We can assume that Beethoven never spoke to him again.

Eight albums, which represent much of the best literature and favorite selections for the violin. They will challenge and delight the performer. Your accompaniment, the Stuttgart Symphony Orchestra conducted by Emil Kahn. The solo parts are performed by the noted American violinist, Geoffrey Applegate.

The Concertmaster   MMO CD 3118/356
Solos from Symphonic Works
Rimsky-Korsakov: Capriccio Espagnol (Alborada)(Fandango), Asturiano **Mozart:** Haffner Serenade (Andante) **Tchaikovsky:** Mozartiana, Swan Lake, Scene No.4 (Andante Non Troppo) **Schumann:** Symphony No. 4 **Offenbach:** Overture To Orpheus In Underworld (Allegro Vivace) **Brahms:** Symphony No. 1 (Andante Sostenuto) **Saint-Saens:** Danse Macabre

Favorite Violin Encores with Orchestra
MMO CD 3119/5021
Bach: Air On The G String **Beethoven:** Minuett In G **Schumann:** Traumerei **Schubert:** Serenade **Raff:** Cavatine, Opus 85 No. 3 **Mozart:** Minuet Divertimento Kv 334 **Godard:** Berceuse **Dvorak:** Humoreske **Brahms:** Hungarian Dance No. 5

Concert Pieces for the Serious Violinist
MMO CD 3120/5022
Massenet: Meditation (From Thais) **Wieniawski:** Legende, Opus 17 **Hubay:** Hejre Kati **Mozart:** Serenade No. 7 Rondo K250 **Beriot:** Scene de Ballet

Eighteenth Century Violin Music
MMO CD 3121/5026
Handel: Largo **Boccherini:** Minuett (Quintet In E, Moderato) **Giordani:** Caro Mio Ben (Larghetto) **Gossec:** Gavotte (Allegro); Siciliana **Pergolesi:** Nina (Andantino) **Haydn:** Serenade (Andante Cantabile) **Handel:** Concerto Grosso No. 12

Violin Favorites with Orchestra Vol. I (Easy)
MMO CD 3122/5027
Offenbach: Barcarolle, Tales of Hoffman (Moderato) **Stephen Foster:** Drink To Me Only With Thine Eyes **Traditional:** Old Folks at Home **Franz Gruber:** Silent Night **Rimsky-Korsakov:** Songs of India **Tchaikovsky:** Chanson Triste **Yradier:** La Paloma **Bizet:** Adagietto, L'arlesienne Suite **Franz Lehar:** Vilja

Violin Favorites with Orchestra Vol. 2
(Moderate)   MMO CD 3123/5028
Mozart: Deh Vieni Non Tardar (Marriage of Figaro) **Verdi:** Questo O Quella (Rigoletto) **Irish Traditional:** Garry Owen, Irish Washer Woman **Scottish Traditional:** The Campbells are Coming **Delibes:** Pizzicato (Sylvia) **Grieg:** Ich Liebe Dich, Anita's Dance **Puccini:** Cho-Cho San's Entrance **Wagner:** Albumblatt **Johann Strauss:** Alfred's Song (Die Fledermaus), Adele's Song

Violin Favorites with Orchestra Vol. 3
(Mod. Diff.)   MMO CD 3124/5029
Telemann: Concerto in A Minor **Francois Shubert:** L'Abeille (The Bee) **Tchaikovsky:** Canzonette (Violin Concerto) **Wagner:** Walter's Prize Song (Der Meistersinger);**Wieniawski:** Kujawiak; **Cui:** Orientale; **Strauss:** Czardas

The Three B's: Bach/Beethoven/Brahms
MMO CD 3125/5041

Best loved melodies arranged for strings and orchestra.

Bach: Arioso "Sleepers Awake," Come Sweet Death, Gigue **Beethoven:** Moonlight Sonata, Prometheus, In God's Honor **Brahms:** Three Waltzes, Lullaby, Hungarian Dance No.1.

Haydn Quartet No.6 in Eb major, Opus 76
MMO CD 3136/503

These string quartets, Opus 76, Nos.1 to 6, were written in 1797-8, during Haydn's last period of composition. They are quite expressive, with delightful touches. The second quartet contains the 'witches minuet' in which the violins, in octaves, lead with a rather spooky tune that is then imitated by the lower instruments, making quite an unearthly canon.

The third is the well-known "Emperor" quartet. Its theme and variations subject of the slow movement, derives from a Croatian folk melody and was commissioned to be the Austrian National Anthem or "Emperor's Hymn." It became Haydn's personal favorite tune. The fourth quartet is popularly known as the "Sunrise" because, in the opening Allegro, the first violin rises slowly out of the sustained harmonies of its accompaniment to announce the principal theme — just as the sun rises out of the East, as it were. The fifth in D, is of haunting beauty. The sixth quartet in Eb introduces a witty trio utilizing the Eb major scale throughout, ascending and descending with the most inventive counterpoint.

Dvorak String Trio "Terzetto," OP.74
2 violins/viola
MMO CD 3143/42

> *"Thank you for continuing to supply the quality music that helps my students perform to their best and rank highly in competitions"*
>
> Diana N.
> Mansura, Louisianna

Vivaldi Concerti in Am, D, Am Opus 3
No. 6,9 8
MMO CD 3126/360

Vivaldi "The Four Seasons"
(2 CD set) $29.98   **MMO CD 3127/361**

Vivaldi "La Tempesta di Mare" Opus 8, No. 5
Albinoni Violin Concerto in A
MMO CD 3128/362

Vivaldi Violin Concerto Opus 3, No. 12
Opus 8, No. 6   **MMO CD 3129/363**

Schubert: Three Sonatinas, Opus 137
MMO CD 3130/5011

These charming sonatinas, written when the composer was 19, are among the most popular of MMO's violin offerings, judging by comments we have received over the years. It is our pleasure to present these to you on compact disc.

Robert Zubrycki, Soloist

Haydn Quartet No.1 in G, Opus 76
MMO CD 3131/501

Haydn Quartet No.2 in D Minor, Opus 76
MMO CD 3132/501

Haydn Quartet No. 3 in C, Opus 76
"Emperor"   **MMO CD 3133/502**

Haydn Quartet No. 4 in Bb major, Opus 76
"Sunrise"   **MMO CD 3134/502**

Haydn Quartet No. 5 in D major, Opus 76
MMO CD 3135/503

Student Editions

Beautiful Music for Two Violins
1st position, vol.1   **MMO CD 3137/5033**

Beautiful Music for Two Violins
2nd position, vol.2   **MMO CD 3138/5038**

Beautiful Music for Two Violins
3rd position, vol.3   **MMO CD 3139/5039**

Beautiful Music for Two Violins
1st, 2nd, 3rd position, vol.4   **MMO CD3140/5040**

Lovely folk tunes and selections from the classics, chosen for their melodic beauty and technical value. They have been skillfully transcribed and edited by Samuel Applebaum, one of America's foremost teachers.

Teacher's Partner: Basic Violin Studies
1st year   **MMO CD 3142/TP6**

Flute

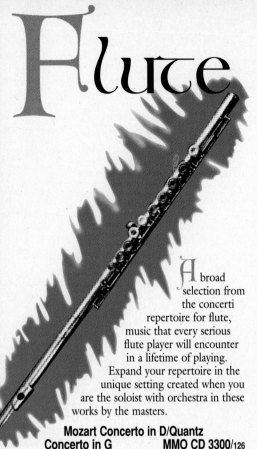

A broad selection from the concerti repertoire for flute, music that every serious flute player will encounter in a lifetime of playing. Expand your repertoire in the unique setting created when you are the soloist with orchestra in these works by the masters.

Mozart Concerto in D/Quantz Concerto in G   MMO CD 3300/126

Mozart Flute Concerto in G major   MMO CD 3301/112

J. S. Bach Suite No. 2 in B minor   MMO CD 3302/127

Boccherini/Vivaldi Concerti/Mozart Andante   MMO CD 3303/142

Haydn/Vivaldi/Frederick "The Great" Concerti   MMO CD 3304/141

Vivaldi/Telemann/Leclair Flute Concerti   MMO CD 3305/350

Bach Brandenburg No. 2/Haydn Concerto   MMO CD 3306/164

Bach Triple Concerto/ Vivaldi Concerto No. 9   MMO CD 3307/166

Mozart/Stamitz Flute Quartets   MMO CD 3308/167

Haydn London Trios   MMO CD 3309/5042

J.S. Bach Brandenburg Concerti No. 4 and No. 5   MMO CD 3310/138

Mozart Three Flute Quartets MMO CD 3311/106

Telemann Am Suite/Gluck "Orpheus" Scene Pergolesi Con. in G (2 CD Set)   MMO CD 3312/110

Flute Song: Easy Familiar Classics   MMO CD 3313/32

A charming program of easily familiar classics orchestrated for a full symphony orchestra and minus the solo melody part, your flute.

J.S.Bach: Air On A G String **Schumann:** Traumerei **Mozart:** Minuet Divertimento **Godard:** Berceuse **Brahms:** Hungarian Dance No .5 **Beethoven:** Minuet in G **Schubert:** Serenade **Raff:** Cavatine, Op .85 **Dvorak:** Humoreske.
The Stuttgart Festival Orchestra, Emil Kahn, Conductor.

Vivaldi 3 Flute Concerti RV 427, 438, Opus 10 No.5   **MMO CD 3314**/365

Vivaldi 3 Flute Concerti RV 440, Opus 10 No.4, RV429   **MMO CD 3315**/366

Easy Solos   Student Editions
Beginning Level Vol.1   **MMO CD 3316**/7020
44 selections chosen for their simplicity of performance. Ideal for the student beginner, these present some challenges and are a perfect introduction to the broad repertoire for the flute, available to players at all levels.

Adios Muchachos; After the Ball; Ah, So Pure; American Patrol; America; Battle Hymn; The Band Played On; Beautiful Isle; Because; Daisy Bell; Eli, Eli; El Chocio; Fantasie Impromptu; Finlandia; Fur Elise; Glow Worm; Gypsy Love; Hatikvoh; Holy City; I Love You Truly; I'll SIng Thee Songs of Araby; In Old Madrid; Just A-wearyin' For You; Kathleen Mavourneen; Kentucky Babe; La Cumparsita; La Paloma; La Spagnola; March Slav; Mexican Hat Dance; Might Lak' a Rose; Oh Promise Me; O Sole Mio!; Pomp and Circumstance; Red River Valley; The Rosary; Santa Lucia; Serenade (V. Herbert); Song of India; Sweet Rosy O'Grady; Rachmaninoff Piano Concerto; To a Wild Rose; Villa; Who is Sylvia?

Easy Solos,   Student Editions,
Beginning Level Vol.2   **MMO CD 3317**/7025
Thirty eight songs with piano accompaniment performed by Harriet Wingreen, staff pianist of the New York Philharmonic.

Ain't Gonna Study War No More; Berceuse; Black Is The Color; Bluebeard; Blues in Eb; Careless Love **Bach:** Chorale No.83; Cradle Song; Far Above Cayuga's Waters; Fireball Polka; Greensleeves; Hello Ma Baby; High School Cadets; H.M.S. Pinafore; In Dulci Jubilo **Bach:** Jesu, Joy Of Man's Desiring; Little Brown Jug; **Sousa:** Manhattan Beach **Borodin:** Melody Prince Igor (Moderato); Mr.Frog Went A Courtin'!; Nocturne; Old Paint; On Top of Old Smoky; Peter and the Wolf; Recruiting Song **Sousa:** Rifle Regiment; Scheherazade; The Sidewalks of New York; Spanish Guitar **Sousa:** Stars & Stripes; The Cossack; Theme from Moldau; **Bizet:** Toreador Song; Valse Noble; When I Was Single; When The Saints Go Marchin' In; You Tell Me Your Dreams; Young Prince & Princess

Easy Jazz Duets   Student Editions
1-3 years   **MMO CD 3318**/4053/4058
Jazz duets: with the 1st part on the left channel and the 2nd part on the right channel. Listen to the duets as played by virtuoso Romeo Penque with rhythm section. Then by lowering the volume level of either channel you can eliminate one flute and play along.

The Rhythm Section: George Duvivier, bass; Bobby Donaldson, drums

Two collections for Flute and Guitar conceived and produced by noted guitarist/lutenist Ed Flower. They provide a broad range of musical experience spanning many centuries of music for the two instruments. Mr. Flower accompanies Jeremy Barlow on flute in each duet. Then thru the magic of split-channel stereo, you can play the flute part accompanied by Ed Flower. A unique opportunity to become part of perhaps the most felicitious grouping in music, the flute and guitar.

Flute And Guitar Duets Vol.1   MMO CD 3319/189
Greensleeves **Finger:** Division on a Ground; Faronell's Ground; **Baron:** Sonata in G major; **Dowland:** If My Complaints **Pilkington:** Rest Sweet Nymphs **Bach:** Sonata in C, BWV.1033 **Couperin:** Soeur Monique; **Vivaldi:** Andante

Flute And Guitar Duets Vol.2   MMO CD 3320/190
Giuliani: Grand Sonata for Flute and Guitar **Faure:** Sicilienne **Ibert:** Entr'acte **Villa-Lobos:** Bachianas Brasileiras No.5; Distribution of the Flowers **Schubert:** An die Musik

First Chair Flute Solos   MMO CD 3333/135
Orchestral accompaniments
Richard Wyton, Soloist

Basic Studies for the Flute
      MMO CD 3334/TP-1
An album designed for the beginning student facing problems of tone, rhythm and articulation. In presenting a professional model, this recording is best introduced as soon as the student has started scales or has progressed in his method book to where review will help solidify his basic technique and sustain his interest in practicing. Practice becomes exciting and rewarding with this approach.

The Joy of the Woodwind Quintets
      MMO CD 3335/145/151
Beethoven: Quintet, Op. 71; **Colomer:** Bouree; **Haydn:** Minuet & Presto ; **Lefebvre:** Finale, Suite Op. 57 ; **Mozart:** German Dance; **Barthe:** Passacaille; **Haydn:** Divertimento ; **Lefebvre:** Suite for Winds

Jewels for Woodwind Quintet
      MMO CD 3336/156/168
Haydn: Introduction & Allegro ; **Mozart:** Menuet, K 421; **Deslandres:** Allegro ; **Danzi:** Quintet in G minor, Op. 56 #2; **Colomer:** Menuet; **Bach:** Andante and Dulci Jubilo; **Koepke:** Rustic Holiday; **Mozart:** Andante & Contradanse K 213; Klughardt, Op. 79; Allegro Molto, K 270; **Balay:** Petite Suite

Bolling Suite for Flute & Jazz Piano Trio
      MMO CD 3342
Baroque and Blue; Sentimentale; Javanaise; Fugace; Irlandaise; Versatile; Véloce

This Suite when first introduced, was performed by Claude Bolling and Jean Pierre Rampal. It swiftly became the most successful Chamber Music recording in history with over one-half million copies purchased. We are delighted to make it available to the pianists and flutists in our MMO family of musicians. *Claude Bolling, himself, has endorsed this recording*

Laureate Series Contest Solos

A new series from MMO featuring the choicest repertoire for the instrument as performed by the foremost players in the land and then by YOU. Graded for easy choice. Each album comes with completely annotated solo part, cues and suggestions for performance.

Beginning Level   **MMO CD 3321**/8001
Gretchaninoff: First Waltz Hopkins: Wanton Waltz and Flirtations Fancy Lewallen: Poeme Petite de Lully: Dances for the King Mozart: Adagio Schubert: Three Themes
Murray Panitz, Philadelphia Orch.

Beginning Level   **MMO CD 3322**/8002
Gossec: Gavotte Hindemith: Echo Kahlau: Menuet Lewallen: Andantino Marpurg: Rondo Sumerlin: Serenade Tailleferre: Pastorale
Donald Peck - Chicago Symphony

Intermediate Level   **MMO CD 3323**/8003
Handel: Sonata No. 5 in F Pessard: Andalouse Telemann: Sonata No. 7 in C Minor (lst mvt.)
Julius Baker, N.Y. Philharmonic

Intermediate Level   **MMO CD 3324**/8004
Bach: Suite in B Minor (Polonaise & Bardinerie) Baksa: Aria de Capo Marcello: Sonata in F; Widor:Scheno
Donald Peck - Chicago Symphony

Advanced Level   **MMO CD 3325**/8005
Bach: Sonata No. 2 in Eb (1st & 2nd mvts) Hindemith: Sonata (1st mvt.) Mozart: Concerto No. 2 in D, K.314 (1st mvt.)
Murray Panitz, Philadelphia Orch.

Advanced Level   **MMO CD 3326**/8006
Bach: Sonata No. 7 in G Minor (1st mvt.) Faure: Concerto No. 1 in G., K. 313, (1st mvt.)
Julius Baker, N.Y. Philharmonic

Intermediate Level   **MMO CD 3327**/8007
Andersen: Schenino Gluck: Minuet and Dance of the Blessed Spirits Handel: Sonata No. 3 in G (1st & 2nd mvts.) Lane: Sonata (1st mvt.) Mozart: Andante in C, K 315
Donald Peck - Chicago Symphony

Advanced Level   **MMO CD 3328**/8008
Handel: Sonata No. 2 in G Minor (1st & 4th mvts.) Henze: Sonatine (1st mvt.) Quantz: Concerto in G (1st mvt.) Telemann: Suite in A Minor ('Les Plaisirs')
Murray Panitz, Philadelphia Orch.

Advanced Level   **MMO CD 3329**/8009
Bach:Arioso Faure: Sicilienne Godard: Idylle Platti: Sonata No. 2 in G (3rd & 4th mvts.)
Julius Baker, N.Y. Philharmonic

Beginning Level   **MMO CD 3330**/8101
Bartok: Evening in the Country Berlioz: Three Songs (King of Thule, Mephistopheles' Serenade and Faust's Air) Ibert: Histoires (Crystal Cage, Leader of the Gold Tortoise, and Little White Donkey) Sibelius: Nocturne
Doriot Dwyer, Boston Symphony

Intermediate Level   **MMO CD 3331**/8104
Avschalomoff: Disconsolate Muse Haydn: Adagio; Martinon: Sonatine; Mendelssohn: Song Without Words, Op. 62, No. 1 and Song Without Words, Op.102, No. 3
Doriot Dwyer, Boston Symphony

Advanced Level   **MMO CD 3332**/8107
Dutilleux: Sonatine Piston: Sonata
Doriot Dwyer, Boston Symphony

> *"When I taught at the high school level, I used your tapes with my band.*
>
> *Now in the process of writing a new textbook for my college bands method, I plan to include a specific recommendation about your series."*
>
> Lynn C
> Wilmore, Kentucky

Recorder

Folk Songs Of Many Nations
MMO CD 3337/202

A method compiled and edited by Erich Katz, Dean of the American Recorder movement and the man responsible for the enormous recorder renaissance in the U.S.A. during the 60's and 70's. Here is a super course for learning to play the soprano recorder. Each lesson is built around a series of duets and trios, beginning with the simplest of folk songs to more elaborate music of Bach. Your fellow player is LaNoue Davenport, recorder virtuoso and former performer with the acclaimed Noah Greenberg Pro Musica group.

Let's Play the Recorder: A Method for Children
MMO CD 3338/220

Here's a delightful approach to recorder study for children. Easily learned exercises, plus fully illustrated hand positions and photographs take the younger player through all the steps necessary to learn this extraordinary instrument.

You Can Play the Recorder: Adult Beginner's Method **MMO CD 3339**

Recorder, guitar, percussion plus bass accompany you. This method, and it's sister edition, above, was developed by Sonya and Gerald Burakoff, two noted teachers of the recorder, who have literally taught thousands to play this early and esteemed instrument, the immediate predecessor to the flute. Album contains a step-by-step instruction course with clearly illustrated text containing photographs and diagrams. Familiar songs and duets guide you to becoming proficient.

Three Sonatas for Flute, Harpsicord & Viola da Gamba **MMO CD 3340**/206

Three Sonatas for Alto Recorder
MMO CD 3341/207

Clarinet

Mozart Clarinet Concerto in A, K.622
A/Bb parts incl.   MMO CD 3201/115

Mozart did not make extensive use of the clarinet until comparitively late in his career, but he wrote exquisitely for the instrument, and the two scores dedicated to his friend, Anton Stadler – the Quintet, K.581 and the Concerto K.622 – are among his most beautiful works. Both, incidentally, belong to the final year of his life. The Clarinet Concerto is in the conventional three movements, with music that transcends conventionality in its remarkable sense of repose and serenity, and what Bernhard Paumgartner has called "Its incredible warmth of tone, perfect balance and unmatched perfection of style." This most popular and widely performed of all the concerti for clarinet is here given a rousing rendition by the Stuttgart Orchestra conducted by Emil Kahn with Keith Dwyer as soloist.

Weber Clarinet Concerto No.1 in F minor, Op.73/Stamitz Clarinet Concerto No.3 in Bb major   MMO CD 3202/162

No composer likes to write music without feeling that an artist exists both capable of, and willing to play it to good advantage. When Carl Maria von Weber met Heinrich Joseph Baermann, one of the greatest clarinetists of the early 19th century, he delightedly began writing all sorts of work for him, including several chamber pieces and the two Clarinet Concertos. In the F minor, it is clear that Weber knew the virtuosity of his player – he makes the soloist range over the entire compass of his instrument, and such quiet moments as do occur are invariably surrounded by runs, leaps and passage work of the utmost brilliance.

Spohr Clarinet Concerto No.1 in C minor, Op.26   MMO CD 3203/163

Ludwig Spohr, who created quite a stir when he began conducting with an odd contraption known as a baton, was also one of the best known violinists of his day (i.e. the first half of the 19th century), and is primarily known today for his concertos and other solo works for the fiddle. That he was also quite adept at writing for other instruments than his own is proved by the C minor Clarinet Concerto, a work a bit low on originality perhaps but one high on wit and solidity of craftsmanship.

Weber: Clarinet Concertino Op.26
Beethoven: Trio for Piano, Violin and Cello, Op.11   MMO CD 3204/114

First Chair Clarinet Solos
Orchestral Excerpts
MMO CD 3205/133

Here are two programmes drawn from the extensive orchestral literature available on MMO records, which feature solo clarinet roles. These are the pieces that the clarinetist will encounter at each stage of his advancement in learning the vast repertoire for the clarinet, in symphonic music.

Beethoven: Symphony No.2, 2nd Mvt. 1st Excerpt, 2nd Excerpt **Weber:** Overture From "Der Freischutz" **Brahms:** Symphony No. 3 In F, 1st Mvt. Excerpt, 2nd Mvt. Excerpt **Mozart:** March No. 1, K.408 **Schubert:** Unfinished Symphony No. 8 In B Minor, 1st Mvt, 2nd Mvt **Tchaikovsky:** Hebrides Overture, Symphony No. 5, 1st Mvt **Mendelssohn:** Fingal's Cave Excerpt **Beethoven:** Country Dance No. 1, No. 2, No. 3

The Art Of The Solo Clarinet
Orchestral Excerpts   MMO CD 3206/134

Mozart: Symphony No 39, In Eb , K543, Excerpt, Trio-Menuetto, Excerpt **Mendelssohn:** Symphony No.3 (Scottish), 1st Mvt., Excerpt, 2nd Mvt., Excerpt **Brahms:** Symphony No. 1 In C Minor, 3rd Mvt **Schubert:** Marche Militaire **Beethoven:** Symphony No. 6 "Pastoral" 2nd Mvt., Excerpt **Wagner:** Siegfried Idyll - 1st Excerpt, 2nd Excerpt **Tchaikovsky:** Nutcracker Suite - Arabian Dance, Waltz of the Flowers **Brahms:** Haydn Variations

Stanley Drucker, N.Y. Philharmonic

Mozart: Quintet for Clarinet and Strings in A, K.581   MMO CD 3207/71

Written for his friend and fellow Mason in Vienna, Anton Stadler, the quintet was completed in September of 1789 and premiered a few days before Christmas of that year. It is one of Mozart's most perfect accomplishments – a score of proud serenity, transparent texture and radiant beauty. It is also an example of Mozart's uncanny ability to combine the best parts of chamber music and concerto music. The solo clarinet leads the ensemble but does not subjugate it. There is an infinite variety of interplay between the performing partners, and all five instruments undertake the virtuoso's role at one time or another. "The result," says Homer Ulrich, "is a piece of music whose charm and delicacy are difficult to duplicate in the literature of strings and winds."

Brahms: Sonatas Opus 120 Nos. 1 & 2   MMO CD 3208/176/177

Brahms wrote these two sonatas for clarinet and piano. Favorites of clarinetists everywhere, they appear, one or the other on recital programs featuring this instrument. With this recording you can hear the piece performed by a young American virtuoso, and then play them with the self-same accompanist.

Jerome Bunke, Clarinetist; Hidemitsu Hayashi, Pianist

Weber: Grand Duo Concertant/
Wagner: Adagio   MMO CD 3209/178

Schumann Fantasy Pieces, Three Romances   MMO CD 3210/179

Beginning level collection of diverse 19th century pieces.

Easy Clarinet Solos   MMO CD 3211/7021
Student Editions 1-3 years

Fearis: Beautiful Isle Of Somewhere **Macdowell:** To a Wild Rose **Dacre:** Daisy Bell **Nugent:** Sweet Rosie O'Grady **Elgar:** Pomp And Circumstance **Nevin:** Mighty Lak' a Rose **Geibel:** Kentucky Babe **Ward:** The Band Played On **Harris:** After the Ball **Neapolitan Song:** Santa Lucia **Cowboy Song:** Red River Valley **Crouch:** Kathleen Mavourneen **Ward:** America the Beautiful **Hebrew Nat'l Anthem: Hatikvoh Meacham:** American Patrol **Howe:** Battle Hymn of the Republic **Clay:** I'll Sing Thee Songs of Araby **Trotere:** In Old Madrid **Di Capua:** O Sole Mio! **Yradier:** La Paloma **Di Chiara:** La Spagnola **Rodriguez:** La Cumparsita **Sanders:** Adios Muchachos **Willard:** El Choclo **De Koven:** O Promise Me **D'hardelot:** Because **Nevin:** The Rosary **Jacobs-Bond:** Just A - Wearyin' For You, I Love You Truly **Lehar:** Vilja (From The Merry Widow) **Adams:** The Holy City **Herbert:** Gypsy Love Song (The Fortune Teller) **Tchaikovsky:** Marche Slave **Von Flotow:** Ah! So Pure (Ach So Fromm From "Martha") **Hebrew Melody:** Eili, Eili **Schubert:** Who Is Sylvia? **Grieg:** Theme (Concerto Opus 16) **Rimsky-Korsakoff:** Song of India **Herbert:** Serenade **Sibelius:** Finlandia **Rachmaninoff:** Theme from Concerto No.2 Opus 18 **Beethoven:** Fur Elise **Chopin:** Fantasie Impromptu **Partichela:** Mexican Hat Dance **Lincke:** The Glow Worm

Easy Clarinet Solos   MMO CD 3212/7026
Student Editions 1-3 years Volume 2

Traditional: I Ain't Gonna Study War No More, On Top Of Old Smoky, Mr. Frog Went A Courting, When I Was Single, Old Paint, Careless Love, Black Is The Color Of My True Love's Hair, When The Saints Go Marching In **Lawlor:** The Sidewalks Of New York **Brahms:** Cradle Song **Strauss:** Fireproof Polka **Folk Song:** Greensleeves **Daniels:** You Tell Me Your Dream **Thompson:** Far Above Cayuga's Waters **College Song:** Spanish Guitar **Eastburn:** Little Brown Jug **Arnold:** Blues In Eb **Howard And Emerson:** Hello! Ma Baby **Bach:** Jesu, Joy Of Man's Desiring **Sullivan:** H.M.S. Pinafore **Prokofieff:** Peter And The Wolf **Sousa:** The High School Cadets, Manhattan Beach, The Rifle Regiment; **Traditional Russian:** The Cossack **Strauss:** Recruiting Song **Smetana:** Theme From "Die Moldau" **Borodin:** Melody From "Prince Igor" **Rimsky-Korsakov:** The Young Prince And The Young Princess **Offenbach:** Scene From "Blue Beard" **Schumann:** Scheherazade **Sousa:** The Stars And Stripes Forever **Bizet:** Toreador's Song **Stravinsky:** Berceuse **Mendelssohn:** Nocturne **Brahms:** Moderato Con Moto **Schubert:** Valse Noble **Bach:** In Dulci Jubilo **Bach:** Chorale No.83

Easy Jazz Duets   MMO CD 3213/4050/4055
Student Editions 1-3 years

A delightful collection of easy to medium duets featuring you plus an all-star fellow instrumentalist, clarinetist Kenny Davern and rhythm section. For the 1st, 2nd, 3rd and 4th year student. You hear both parts played in stereo, then each duet is repeated with first the 1st part omitted and then the 2nd part, so you can play along.

Geo. Duvivier, bass; Bobby Donaldson, drums

Laureate Series Contest Solos

Clarinetists will derive both pleasure and learning when using these recordings. They feature some of the most talented soloists, first chair players with major orchestras. Each piece is performed by the soloist, then the accompaniment is provided for the at-home player. The compositions are all drawn from widely used State Contest Pieces, and graded for each level. The scores are annotated by the soloist. Suggestions for their performance are included. A Master Class!

Beginning Leve Vol. 1   MMO CD 3221/8011
Buchtel: Serenade **Edmunds:** Lament **Frangkiser:** Capricious Imp **Gretchaninoff:** Suite Miniature (1 & 5) **Hovey-Leonard:** Song of Spring **Kennaway:** Caprice **Langenus:** Lullaby **MacDowell:** To A Wild Rose.
Jerome Bunke, Clinician

Beginning Level Vol. 2   MMO CD 3222/8012
Baermann: Adagio (Etude No. 24) **Hovey-Leonard:** Chanson Moderne **Langenus:** Chrysalis **Mozart:** Minuet and Trio, K.361 **Stamitz:** Concerto No. 3 in Bb (Romance) **Weinberger:** Sonatine I, II and III.
Harold Wright, Boston Symphony

Intermediate Level Vol.1   MMO CD 3223/8013
Aubert: Aria and Presto **Frank:** Evening Piece **Mozart:** Minuet, K. 334 **Pierne:** Piece in G Minor **Schumann:** Fantasy Piece No. 1 **Stamitz:** Concerto 3 in Bb (Rondo).
Stanley Drucker, N.Y. Philharmonic

Intermediate Level Vol.2   MMO CD 3224/8014
Delmas: Promenade **Tuthil:** Chip's Piece and Chip's Fast Piece **Wagner:** Adagio **Wanhal:**Sonata (3rd mvt.)
Jerome Bunke, Clinician

Advanced Level Vol.1   MMO CD 3225/8015
Mozart: Concerto in A., K. 622 (3rd mvt.) **Hindemith:** Sonate (2nd S 4th mvts.) **Brahms:** Sonata, F. min. Op. 120. No. 1.
Stanley Drucker, N.Y. Philharmonic

Advanced Level Vol.2   MMO CD 3226/8016
Mozart: Concerto in A., K. 622 (1st mvt.) **Rabaud:** Solos de Concours.
Harold Wright, Boston Symphony

Intermediate Level Vol.3   MMO CD 3227/8017
Mozart: Concerto in A., K. 622 (2nd mvt.) **Wilson:** Sonatina **Williams:** Studies in English Folksong.
Stanley Drucker, N.Y. Philharmonic

Advanced Level Vol.3   MMO CD 3228/8018
Brahms: Sonata in E, Op. 120 No. 2 (1st mvt.) **Cavallini:** Adagio and Tarantella **Dello Joio:** Conversance (Tema, Var. No.2); **Weber:** Concerto in E Minor
Stanley Drucker, N.Y. Philharmonic

Advanced Level Vol.4   MMO CD 3229/8019
Brahms: Sonata in F Minor, Op.120, No. 1 (1st & 2nd mvts.) **Weber:** Concerto in Eb, Op. 74 (2nd & 3rd mvts.).
Harold Wright, Boston Symphony

Brahms Quintet in Bm, Op.115 MMO CD 3230/61

The Teacher's Partner–Basic Studies
                                    MMO CD 3231/TP2
Scales in varied articulations, solos and duets with piano accompaniment. Covers first year of study and *can be used with any method book*. It addresses problems of pitch, rhythm, tone and articulation, presenting a professional model.

Jewels for Woodwind Quintet
                            MMO CD 3232/147/153
Beethoven: Quintet, Op. 71 **Colomer:** Bouree **Haydn:** Minuet & Presto **Lefebvre:** Finale, Suite Op.5 **Mozart:** German Dance **Barthe:** Passacaille **Haydn:** Divertimento **Lefebvre:** Suite for Winds **Reid:** Woodwind Suite in Eb

Masterpieces for Woodwind Quintet
                            MMO CD 3233/158/171
Haydn: Introduction & Allegro **Mozart:** Menuet, K 421 **Deslandres:** Allegro **Danzi:** Quintet in G minor, Op. 56 #2 **Colomer:** Menuet **Bach:** Andante in Dulci Jubilo **Koepke:** Rustic Holiday **Mozart:** Andante & Contradanse K 213; Andante Grazioso (Qt. Op. 79); Allegro Molto, K 270 **Balay:** Petite Suite

From Dixie to Swing   MMO CD 3234/4090
Standards from the Dixie and Swing eras, performed by six classic players assembled for this recording by arranger pianist Dick Wellstood; "Doc" Cheatham, trumpet; Vic Dickenson, trombone; Kenny Davern, clarinet and soprano sax; George Duvivier, bass and Gus Johnson, Jr., drums.
Way Down Yonder in New Orleans; Sunny Side of the Street; Second Hand Rose; Exactly Like You; Rose of Washington Square; I Want a Little Girl; Red Sails in the Sunset; The Royal Garden Blues
Great tunes, great players, great fun!

20 Dixie Classics   MMO CD 3824/4021
(See pg 14 trumpet for details)

20 Rhythm Backgrounds to Standards
(See pg 14 trumpet for details) MMO CD 3825/4021

Carl Baermann's Method for Clarinet
Here's a landmark recording of the entire Carl Baermann Method for Clarinet, the original and still most authoritative technical study for the instrument.
These two volumes contain the entire Opus 63 and 64 plus extensive notes on performance. Produced by John Cipolla, noted teacher, soloist and recitalist. Mr. Cipolla has spent the better part of two years preparing this material.
He performs each selection, as well as provides the piano accompaniment to each piece. Destined to become a primary tool in teaching and instruction for the clarinet.

The Virtuoso Clarinetist Opus 63
(4CD Set)   MMO CD 3240

The Art of Clarinet Opus 64
(4CD Set)   MMO CD 3241

Oboe

Albinoni Three Oboe Concerti Opus 7 No. 3, No. 6, Opus 9 No. 2   MMO CD 3400

Three Oboe Concerti: Handel, Telemann, Vivaldi   MMO CD 3401/301

Mozart/Stamitz Oboe Quartets in F
K. 370; Opus 8 No. 3   MMO CD 3402/143

J.S. Bach Brandenburg Concerto No. 2, Telemann Concerto in A minor
                                    MMO CD 3403/165
Henry Sargous, our oboe soloist on 3401, 3402 and 3403 has performed as a guest soloist with innumerable orchestras in the United States and Canada on both radio and television. For several seasons, he was principal oboist at the renowned Marlboro Music Festival under the direction of Pablo Casals.

The Oboe Soloist (2 CD Set)
                                    MMO CD 3404/117
Loeillet: Andante & Allegro **Handel:** Concerto No.8 in Bb **Yamada:** Kuruka-Kuruka **Debussy:** Mazurka **Telemann:** Sonata in Am **Bizet:** Sym. in C, 2nd Mvt. **Laurischkus:** Two Arabian Dances **Rachmaninoff:** Vocalise **Bach:** Aira **Wagner:** Dreams **Fasch:** Largo **Schumann:** Romance **Berger:**Toadina **Glière:** Song **Liszt:** Two Songs

Masterpieces for Woodwind Quintet
                            MMO CD 3405/146/152
Beethoven: Quintet, Op. 71 **Colomer:** Bouree **Haydn:** Minuet & Presto **Lefebvre:** Finale, Suite Op.5 **Mozart:** German Dance **Barthe:** Passacaille **Haydn:** Divertimento **Lefebvre:** Suite for Winds **Reid:** Woodwind Suite in Eb

The Joy of Woodwind Quintets
                            MMO CD 3406/157/169
Haydn: Introduction & Allegro **Mozart:** Menuet, K 421 **Deslandres:** Allegro **Danzi:** Quintet in G minor, Op. 56 #2 **Colomer:** Menuet **Bach:** Andante in Dulci Jubilo **Koepke:** Rustic Holiday **Mozart:** Andante & Contradanse K 213; Klughardt,. Op. 79; Allegro Molto, K 270 **Balay:** Petite Suite

Small numbers on far right indicate the cassette edition of each album

Trumpet

3 Trumpet Concerti: Haydn, Telemann, Fasch
MMO CD 3801/6008

Haydn's Concerto is a perennial favorite among trumpeters. Here it is coupled with two equally attractive baroque works. The trumpet parts are performed by Peter Piacquadio, before you perform them. A joy for trumpeters! One of our most popular releases!

The Stuttgart Festival Orch.–Emil Kahn, Conductor

Easy Solos Student Editions
Beginning Level Vol.1   MMO CD 3802/7023
Fearis: Beautiful Isle of Somewhere **Macdowell:** To a Wild Rose **Dacre:** Daisy Bell **Nugent:** Sweet Rosie O'Grady **Elgar:** Pomp and Circumstance **Nevin:** Mighty Lak' a Rose **Geibel:** Kentucky Babe. **Ward:** The Band Played On **Harris:** After the Ball **Neapolitan Song:** Santa Lucia **Cowboy Song:** Red River Valley **Crouch:** Kathleen Mavourneen **Ward:** America the Beautiful **Hebrew Nat'l Anthem:** Hatikvoh **Meacham:** American Patrol **Howe:** Battle Hymn of the Republic **Clay:** I'll Sing thee Songs of Araby **Trotere:** In Old Madrid **Di Capua:** O Sole Mio! **Yradier:** La Paloma **Di Chiara:** La Spagnola **Rodriguez:** La Cumparsita **Sanders:** Adios Muchachos **Willard:** El Choclo **De Koven:** O Promise Me **D'hardelot:** Because **Nevin:** The Rosary **Jacobs-Bond:** Just A-Wearyin' for You, I Love You Truly **Lehar:** Villa (from the Merry Widow) **Adams:** The Holy City **Herbert:** Gypsy Love Song (The Fortune Teller) **Tchaikovsky:** Marche Slave **Von Flotow:** Ah! So Pure ("Martha") **Hebrew Melody:** Eili, Eili **Schubert:** Who is Sylvia? **Grieg:** Theme (Concerto Opus 16) **Rimsky-Korsakoff:** Song of India **Herbert:** Serenade **Sibelius:** Finlandia **Rachmaninoff:** Theme from Concerto No.2 Opus 18 **Beethoven:** Fur Elise **Chopin:** Fantasie Impromptu **Partichela:** Mexican Hat Dance **Lincke:** The Glow Worm

Easy Solos Student Editions
Beginning Level Vol.2   MMO CD 3803/7028
I Ain't Gonna Study War No More; On Top of Old Smoky; Mr. Frog Went a Courting; When I Was Single; Old Paint; Careless Love; Black is the Color of My True Love's Hair; When the Saints Go Marching In **Lawlor:** The Sidewalks of New York **Brahms:** Cradle Song **Strauss:** Fireproof Polka **Folk Song:** Greensleeves **Daniels:** You Tell Me Your Dream **Thompson:** Far Above Cayuga's Waters **College Song:** Spanish Guitar **Eastburn:** Little Brown Jug **Arnold:** Blues in Eb; Howard and Emerson: Hello! Ma Baby; Bach: Jesu, Joy of Man's Desiring **Sir Arthur Sullivan:** H.M.S. Pinafore **Prokofieff:** Peter and the Wolf **Sousa:** The High School Cadets, Manhattan Beach, The Rifle Regiment **Traditional Russian:** The Cossack Strauss: Recruiting Song **Smetana:** Theme from "Die Moldau" **Borodin:** Melody from "Prince Igor" **Rimsky-Korsakov:** The Young Prince and the Young Princess **Offenbach:** Scene from "Blue Beard" **Schumann:** Sheherazade **Sousa:** The Stars and Stripes Forever **Bizet:** Toreador's Song **Stravinsky:** Berceuse **Mendelssohn:** Nocturne **Brahms:** Moderato Con Moto **Schubert:** Valse Noble **Bach:** In Dulci Jubilo, Chorale No.83

Easy Jazz Duets with Rhythm Section
Beginning Level   MMO CD3804/4054/4059

A delightful collection of easy to medium duets featuring you plus an all-star instrumentalist, trumpeter Burt Collins, and rhythm section. For the 1st, 2nd, 3rd and 4th year student. You hear both parts played in stereo, then each duet is repeated with first the 1st part omitted and then the 2nd part omitted, so you can play along .

Music for Brass Ensemble MMO CD 3805/6001

A superior collection of brass classics, performed by the Classic Brass Ensemble. A very broad program of material designed to test the abilities of the average through excellent trumpeter. Peter Piacquadio, trumpet soloist shows the way and then you are at stage center.

Reiche: Sonata No.19 (Moderato) (Adagio) **Pezel:** Intrade, Sarabande, Bal, Gigue, Sonata No.2, /Sonat For Die Bankelsangerlieder, Sonata No.22 **Gabrieli:** Canzona Per Sonare No.1 (La Spiritata), Canzona Per Sonare No.2 **Holborne:** Honie-Suckle; Night Watch **Susato:** Ronde, Salterelle, Pavane **Schein:** Paduana & Gaillard

First Chair Trumpet Solos   MMO CD 3806/136
Handel: Watermusic **Wagner:** Overture to Rienzi **Brahms:** Academic Festival Overture **Suppe:** Overture to Light Cavalry **Bruckner:** Symphone No. 3 in Dm **Mendelssohn:** Calm Sea and Prosperous Voyage
The Stuttgart Festival Orch.–Emil Kahn, Conductor

The Art of the Solo Trumpet MMO CD 3807/137
Purcell: Sonata For Trumpet And Strings In D (Allegro) **Stradella:** Sonata For Trumpet And Strings In C **Torelli:** Symphony With Trumpet **Manfredini:** Concerto For Two Trumpets **Bach:** Brandenberg Concerto No. 2

Baroque, Brass and Beyond
MMO CD 3808/6015
Ewald: Opus No. 5 **Bach:** Contrapunctdus V "Art of Fugue," Contrapunctdus I **Palestrina:** Ricercar del Primo Tuono **Brade:** Almand, Gaillard **Franck:** Two Pavans **Pezel:** Sonata No.25 **Handel:** Overture to Berenice-Largo & Allegro **Purcell:** Voluntary on Old 100th **Pezel:** Sonata No.25
The Illinois Brass Quintet

Basic Studies   MMO CD 3820

Scales in varied articulations, solos and duets with piano accompaniment. Covers first year of study and *can be used with any method book.* It addresses problems of pitch, rhythm, tone and articulation, presenting a professional model.

20 Dixie Classics   MMO CD 3824

Maple Leaf Rag; San; Sugar Foot Stomp; Copenhagen; Tin Roof Blues; Farewell Blues; Weary Blues; Why Don't You do Right?; Milenberg Joys; King Porter Stomp; Bugle Call Rag; Wolverine Blues; A Good Man is Hard to Find; After You've Gone; Basin Street Blues; Your Feet's Too Big; The Saints; Floatin' Down to Cotton Town; Do You Know What it Means to Miss New Orleans; Dallas Blues

20 Rhythm Backgrounds to Standards
MMO CD 3825

Tenderly; Basin St. Blues; It's Been a Long, Long Time; Rosetta; Sentimental Journey; After You've Gone; S'posin'; When You're Smiling; Nobody's Sweetheart; Strip Poker; Make Love to Me; Drifting and Dreaming; Enjoy Yourself; Sweetheart of Sigma Chi; Angry; One for My Baby; Dinah; Mister Sandman; There will Never Be Another You; I've Heard that Song Before

Laureate Series Contest Solos

The choicest repertoire for your instrument, here performed by virtuoso soloists, clinicians and first chair performers with the five major orchestras in the United States. Hear each piece performed, than play with the accompaniment provided. An unexcelled teaching and learning situation.

Beginning Level   MMO CD 3811/8031
Bach: Bis du bet mir **Debussy:** Mandoline **Fitzgerald:** English Suite (1st and 3rd mvts.) **Handel:** March **Mozart:** Isis und Osiris **Pergolesi:** Nina **Purcell:** Trumpet Tune **Porret:** Esquisse 1 **Scarlatti:** Sento nel core **Young:** Contempora Suite (Prelude)
Gerard Schwarz, N.Y. Philharmonic

Beginning Level   MMO CD 3812/8032
Bach: Arioso **Bakaleinikoff:** Serenade **Clarke** (Purcell): Trumpet Voluntary **Donaudy:** Two Arias **Fitzgerald:** Italian Suite **Krieger:** Allegro **Tenaglia:** Aria
Armando Ghitalla, Boston Symphony

Intermediate Level   MMO CD 3813/8033
Anderson: A Trumpeter's Lullaby **Bakaleinikoff:** Polonaise **Burke:** The Magic Trumpet **Fitzgerald:** Frolic **Lesur:** Aubade **Prokofiev:** Kije's Wedding **Donaudy:** Aria & Allegro
Robert Nagel, Soloist, NY Brass Ensemble

Intermediate Level   MMO CD 3814/8034
Balay: Petite Piece Concertante **Bernstein:** Rondo for Lifey **Goedicke:** Concert Etude, Op. 49 **Ropartz:** Andante and Allegro **Telemann:** Presto
Gerard Schwarz, N.Y. Philharmonic

Advanced Level   MMO CD 3815/8035
Handel: Aria con Variazioni **L. Mozart:** Concerto **Vivaldi:** Allegro
Robert Nagel, Soloist, NY Brass Ensemble

Intermediate Level   MMO CD 3816/8036
Corelli: Sonata **Vail** (1st and 2nd mvts.) **Purcell:** Sonata (1st and 3rd mvts.) **Webber:** Sonata in F Major
Armando Ghitalla, Boston Symphony

Intermediate Level   MMO CD 3817/8037
Balay: Prelude and Ballade **Goeyens:** All' Antica (Solo in the Ancient Style) **Stravinsky:** Dance of the Ballerina ("Petrouchka") **Whitney:** Concertino (3rd mvt.)
Gerard Schwarz, N.Y. Philharmonic

Advanced Level   MMO CD 3818/8038
Fiocco: Allegro **Hummel:** Concerto (3rd mvt.) **Latham:** Suite **Nagel:** Trumpet Professional
Robert Nagel, Soloist, NY Brass Ensemble

Advanced Level   MMO CD 3819/8039
Haydn: Concerto (2nd and 3rd mvts.) **Hindemith:** Sonate (2nd mvt.) **Holmes:** Sonata (3rd mvt.)
Armando Ghitalla, Boston Symphony

Beginning Level   MMO CD 3820/8131
Bononcini: Per La Gloria D'Adorarri **Clerisse:** Theme Varie **Dedrick:** A Tune for Christopher
Raymond Crisara, Concert Soloist

Beginning Level   MMO CD 3821/8132
Barrow: Scherzo **Granados:** Andaluza **Marteau:** Morceau Vivant **Mendelssohn:** If With All Your Hearts **Mozart:** Allegretto **Whitney:** Concertino (2nd mvt.)
Raymond Crisara, Concert Soloist

Intermediate Level   MMO CD 3822/8134
Balay: Andante et Allegretto **Barat:** Andante et Scherzo **Nestico:** Portrait of a Trumpet **Sanders:** Square Dance
Raymond Crisara, Concert Soloist

Trombone

15

Saxophone

Alto

Easy Solos Student Editions
Beginning Level Vol.1   **MMO CD 4101**/7022

Adios Muchachos; After the Ball; Ah, So Pure; American Patrol; America; Battle Hymn; The Band Played On; Beautiful Isle; Because; Daisy Bell; Eli, Eli; El Chocio; Fantasie Impromptu; Finlandia; Fur Elise; Glow Worm; Gypsy Love; Hatikvoh; Holy City; I Love You Truly; I'll Sing Thee Songs of Araby; In Old Madrid; Just A-Wearyin' for You; Kathleen Mavourneen; Kentucky Babe; La Cumparsita; La Paloma; La Spagnola; March Slav; Mexican Hat Dance; Might Lak' a Rose; Oh Promise Me; O Sole Mio!; Pomp and Circumstance; Red River Valley; The Rosary; Santa Lucia; Serenade (V. Herbert); Song of India; Sweet Rosy O'Grady; Rachmaninoff Piano Concerto; To a Wild Rose; Villa; Who is Sylvia?

Easy Solos Student Editions
Beginning Level Vol.2   **MMO CD 4102**/7027

Ain't Gonna Study War No More; Berceuse; Black is the Color; Bluebeard; Blues in E; Careless Love **Bach:** Chorale No.83; Cradle Song; Far Above Cayuga's Waters; Fireball Polka; Greensleeves; Hello Ma Baby; High School Cadets; H.M.S. Pinafore; In Dulci Jubilo **Bach:** Jesu, Joy of Man's Desiring; Little Brown Jug; **Sousa:** Manhattan Beach; Rifle Regiment; Stars & Stripes; **Borodin:** Melody Prince Igor (Moderato); Mr. Frog went a Courtin'; Nocturne; Old Paint; On Top of Old Smoky; Peter and the Wolf; Recruiting Song Scheherazade; The Sidewalks of New York; Spanish Guitar The Cossack; Theme from Moldau; **Bizet:** Toreador Song; Valse Noble; When I was Single; You Tell Me Your Dreams; Young Prince & Princess; When the Saints Go Marchin' In

Easy Jazz Duets Student Editions
1-3 years   **MMO CD 4103**/4051/4056

Easy to medium duets performed by Hal McKusick, Alto Sax Star, and YOU! Graded for the 1st, 2nd, 3rd and 4th year student, these duets are a joy to hear and play. You're accompanied by the Benny Goodman rhythm section, laying down a bed of great easy-to-follow rhythm tracks. The rhythm section, George Duvivier and Bobby Donaldson, jazz legends.

For Saxes Only   **MMO CD 4104**/4006

Join an All-Star Band as lead Alto or Tenor in arrangements styled after the Basie and Ellington Bands. Tailored for your horn, this album includes Bb and Eb parts plus suggested improvisations. A totally unique experience in playing with a professional sax section, and an absolute must for stage band players.

Conceived and arranged by Bob Wilber

Laureate Series Contest Solos

We had two major virtuoso performers, Paul Brodie of Canada, and Vincent Abato, the legendary American saxophonist, perform these eight albums of selections from the various state contest solo lists. Each artist also provided a commentary in the form of a performance guide.

Beginning Level   **MMO CD 4111**/8021

Bach: Gavotte **Bizet:** Intermezzo **Chopin:** Largo **Dvorak:** Larghetto **Gretchaninoff:** Evening Waltz **Grieg:** Album Leaf **Haydn:** Andante **Kreisler:** Rondino **Mozart:** Ave Verum **Weber:** Hunter's Chorus

Paul Brodie, Canadian Soloist

Beginning Level   **MMO CD 4112**/8022

Borodin: Polovetsian Dance **Mozart:** Minuet **Rameau:** La Vilageoise **Ravel:** Pavane **Tenaglia:** Aria Antica **Young:** contempora Suite (3rd & 4th mvts.)

Vincent Abato, Metropolitan Opera Orch.

Intermediate Level   **MMO CD 4113**/8023

Bach: Andante Cantabile **Beethoven:** Romance **Bizet:** Minuet **Blavet:** Adagio and Gigue **Handel:** Bouree

Paul Brodie, Canadian Soloist

Intermediate Level   **MMO CD 4114**/8024

Bach: Air **D'Ambrosio:** Canzonetta **Francais:** Cinq Danses Exotiques (Mambo. Samba et Merengue) **Mozart:** Sonatina **Musorgsky:** The Old Castle **Platti:** Sonata No. 5 (3rd mvt.)

Vincent Abato, Metropolitan Opera Orch..

Advanced Level   **MMO CD 4115**/8025

Benson: Farewell **Jacob:** Rhapsody **Vivaldi:** Concerto in A Minor (3rd mvt.) **Whitney:** Rhumba

Paul Brodie, Canadian Soloist

Advanced Level   **MMO CD 4116**/8026

Creston: Sonata (2nd & 3rd mvts.) **Rabaud:** Solo de Concours **Schubert:** The Bee

Vincent Abato, Metropolitan Opera Orch.

Advanced Level   **MMO CD 4117**/8027

Jacob: Sonata 1st mvt. **Vivaldi:** Sonata in G Minor **Ward:** An Abstract

Paul Brodie, Canadian Soloist

Advanced Level   **MMO CD 4118**/8028

Eccles: Sonata (1st. 2nd & 4th mvts.) **Gurewich:** Concerto (3rd mvt.) **Handel:** Adagio and Allegro **Heiden:** Sonata (2nd mvt.)

Vincent Abato, Metropolitan Opera Orch..

Blues Fusion   **MMO CD 4105**/4098

Tricky Dicky; When The Spirit; Cocaine Stomp;.Wailer Blues; Boogie Breakdown; Tremblin'; Yancey's Fancy; Mad Dog Blues

Jobim– Brazilian Bossa Nova   **MMO CD 4106**

The Girl From Ipanema; So Danco Samba; Once I Loved; Dindi; One Note Samba; Meditation; How Insensitive; Triste; Quiet Nights Of Quiet Stars; Wave

Teacher's Partner   **MMO CD 4119**

Play Lead in a Sax Section   **MMO CD 4120**

Days of Wine & Roses–Sensual Sax   **MMO CD 4121**

20 Dixie Classics   **MMO CD 4124**

Maple Leaf Rag; San; Sugar Foot Stomp; Copenhagen; Tin Roof Blues; Farewell Blues; Weary Blues; Why Don't You do Right?; Milenberg Joys; King Porter Stomp; Bugle Call Rag; Wolverine Blues; A Good Man is Hard to Find; After You've Gone; Basin Street Blues; Your Feet's Too Big; The Saints; Floatin' Down to Cotton Town; Do You Know What it Means to Miss New Orleans; Dallas Blues

20 Rhythm Backgrounds to Standards
(See Tenor Sax for details)   **MMO CD 4125**

Instructional Methods
See page 7 for details

Evolution of the Blues   **MMO CD 7004**/1008
Clark Terry/Bob Wilber

The Art of Improvisation   **MMO CD 7005**/601
Rich Matteson/Petersen Vol. 1

The Art of Improvisation   **MMO CD 7006**/602
Rich Matteson/Petersen Vol. 2

The Blues Minus You   **MMO CD 7007**/1011
Mal Waldron

Take a Chorus   **MMO CD 7008**
Stan Getz/Jimmy Raney/Hal McKusick/George Duvivier/Ed Shaughnessy

Tenor

Easy Tenor Sax Solos Student Editions
Vol.1, 1-3 years   **MMO CD 4201**/7021

Adios Muchachos; After the Ball; Ah, So Pure; American Patrol; America; Battle Hymn; The Band Played On; Beautiful Isle; Because; Daisy Bell; Eli, Eli; El Chocio; Fantasie Impromptu; Finlandia; Fur Elise; Glow Worm; Gypsy Love; Hatikvoh; Holy City; I Love You Truly; I'll SIng Thee Songs of Araby; In Old Madrid; Just A-Wearyin' for You; Kathleen Mavourneen; Kentucky Babe; La Cumparsita; La Paloma; La Spagnola; March Slav; Mexican Hat Dance; Might Lak' a Rose; Oh Promise Me; O Sole Mio!; Pomp and Circumstance; Red River Valley; The Rosary; Santa Lucia; Serenade (V. Herbert); Song of India; Sweet Rosy O'Grady; Rachmaninoff Piano Concerto; To a Wild Rose; Villa; Who is Sylvia?

Easy Solos Student Editions
Vol.2, 1-3 years   **MMO CD 4202**/7026

Ain't Gonna Study War No More; Berceuse; Black is the Color; Bluebeard; Blues in E; Careless Love **Bach:** Chorale No.83; Cradle Song; Far Above Cayuga's Waters; Fireball Polka; Greensleeves; Hello Ma Baby; High School Cadets; H.M.S. Pinafore; In Dulci Jubilo **Bach:** Jesu, Joy of Man's Desiring; Little Brown Jug; **Sousa:** Manhattan Beach **Borodin:** Melody Prince Igor (Moderato); Mr. Frog Went a Courtin'!; Nocturne; Old Paint; On Top of Old Smoky; Peter and the Wolf; Recruiting Song **Sousa:** Rifle Regiment; Scheherazade; The Sidewalks of New York; Spanish Guitar **Sousa:** Stars & Stripes; The Cossack; Theme from Moldau; **Bizet:** Toreador Song; Valse Noble; When I Was Single; When the Saints Go Marchin' In; You Tell Me Your Dreams; Young Prince & Princess

ℱrench ℌorn

Easy Jazz Duets with Rhythm Section
MMO CD 4203/4052/4057

Duets from the easiest lst year level up through difficult material that would challenge the 2nd, 3rd and 4th year player. Play with jazz icon Zoot Sims, George Duvivier on bass and Bobby Donaldson on drums. These duets will also delight the professional in their simplicity of execution.

For Saxes Only arranged by Bob Wilber
MMO CD 4204/4006

Join an All-Star Band as lead Alto or Tenor in arrangements styled after the Basie and Ellington Bands. Tailored for Alto or Tenor, this album includes Bb and Eb parts plus suggested improvisions. A totally unique experience in playing with professional sax section, and an absolute must for stage band players
Concieved and arranged by Bob Wilber

Blues Fusion
MMO CD 4205/4098
Tricky Dicky; When the Spirit; Cocaine Stomp; Wailer Blues; Boogie Breakdown; Tremblin'; Yancey's Fancy; Mad Dog Blues

Jobim Bossa Nova with Strings
MMO CD 4206
The Girl from Ipanema; So Danco Samba; Once I Loved; Dindi; One Note Samba; Meditation; How Insensitive; Triste; Quiet Nights of Quiet Stars; Wave

20 Dixie Classics
MMO CD 4207
(See Alto Sax for details)

20 Rhythm Backgrounds to Standards
MMO CD 4208
Tenderly; Basin St. Blues; It's Been a Long, Long Time; Rosetta; Sentimental Journey; After You've Gone; S'posin'; When You're Smiling; Nobody's Sweetheart; Strip Poker; Make Love to Me; Drifting and Dreaming; Enjoy Yourself; Sweetheart of Sigma Chi; Angry; One for My Baby; Dinah; Mister Sandman; There will Never be Another You; I've Heard that Song Before

Play Lead in a Sax Section
MMO CD 4209

Days of Wine & Roses–Sensual Sax
MMO CD 4210

Instructional Methods
See page 7 for details

Evolution of the Blues
MMO CD 7004/1008
Clark Terry/Bob Wilber

The Art of Improvisation
MMO CD 7005/601
Rich Matteson/Petersen Vol. 1

The Art of Improvisation
MMO CD 7006/602
Rich Matteson/Petersen Vol. 2

The Blues Minus You
MMO CD 7007/1011
Mal Waldron

Take a Chorus
MMO CD 7008
Stan Getz/Jimmy Raney/Hal McKusick/George Duvivier/Ed Shaughnessy

---

Mozart: Concerti Nos. 2 & 3
K.417, K.447
MMO CD 3501/6020

Two concerti at the top of the horn literature. Performed by every hornist at concerts and on discs, it's Mozart. What more need be said?

Baroque, Brass & Beyond
MMO CD 3502/6016

The superb faculty quintet at the University of Illinois performs an extraordinary program of brass favorites, minus French Horn.
Ewald: Opus No. 5 **Bach:** Contrapunctdus V "Art of Fugue," Contrapunctdus I **Palestrina:** Ricercar del Primo Tuono **Brade:** Almand, Gaillard **Franck:** Two Pavans **Pezel:** Sonata No. 25 **Handel:** Overture to Berenice -Largo & Allegro **Purcell:** Voluntary on Old 100th
Fred Griffen, soloist

Music for Brass Ensemble
MMO CD 3503/6002

A superior collection of brass classics performed by the Classic Brass Players. A broad program designed to test the abilities of the average through excellent horn player.
Reiche: Sonata No.19 **Pezel:** Intrade, Sarabande, Bal, Gigue, Sonata No.2, /Sonata for die Bankelsangerlieder, Sonata No.22 **Gabrieli:** Canzona per Sonare No.1 (La Spiritata), Canzona per Sonare No.2, Sonata No.1 **Storl:** Andante **Holborne:** Honie-Suckle; Night Watch **Susato:** Ronde, Salterelle, Pavane **Schein:** Paduana & Galliard

Mozart Sonatas for Two Horns
MMO CD 3504

French Horn Woodwind Music
MMO CD 3520/149/155

Beethoven: Quintet, Op. 71, Adagio & Allegro; Adagio; Menuetto; Allegro - Rondo **Haydn:** Minuet, Allegretto; **Mozart:** German Dance, Allegro; **Haydn:** Presto, Rondo; **Colomer:** Bourée; **Lefebvre:** Finale, Suite, Opu. 57 **Reiche:** Allegro moderato, Scherzo, Allegro, Andante Grazioso, Finale, Allegro molto **Barthe:** Passacaille, Allegro **Haydn:** Divertimento, Allegro con spirito Andante quasi allegretto Menuetto Allegretto, Rondo **Lefebvre:** Suite for Woodwinds

Masterpieces for Woodwind Quintet
MMO CD 3521/161/173

Mozart: Menuet, K.421, Allegretto **Deslandres:** Piece for Woodwind Quintet, Allegro **Haydn:** Introduction & Allegro for Woodwind Quintet **Danzi:** Woodwind Quintet in G minor, Op. 56 No. 2, Allegretto, Andante, Allegro, Allegro **Colomer:** Menuet, Moderato **C.P.E. Bach:** from Six Sonatas, Andante **Haydn:** from Octet, Menuetto & Trio **Koepke:** Rustic Holiday **Mozart:** from Divertimento No. 8, K.213, Andante, Contredanse **Klughardt:** from Quintet, Op.79, Andante grazioso **Bach:** In Dulci Jubilo **Balay:** Petite Suite Miniature, Menuet, Courte Gavotte, Sarabande, Petit Rondeau **Mozart:** from Divertimento No. 14, K.270,Allegro molto

---

Laureate Series Contest Solos

Listen as these extraordinary virtuosi play each piece. Learn what it means to achieve first chair status with a major orchestra. Music included, plus suggestions for performance.

Beginning Level
MMO CD 3511/8041
Bakaleinikoff: Cavatina **Bartok:** Hungarian Folk Song **Beethoven:** Farewell Song **Chopin:** Cavatina **Frescobaldi:** Gagliardo **Grieg:** To Spring **Nyquist:** Melody for Horn **Mozart:** Non piu totto ascoltai
Mason Jones, Philadelphia Orch.

Beginning Level
MMO CD 3512/8042
Bach: Chorale Prelude **Ballatore:** Serenata **Beethoven:** Little Rondo **Cohen:** Legend of the Hills **Ilyinsky:** Lullaby **Kaplan:** Soliloquy **Poole:** Song of a City **Purcell:** Minuet **Schubert:** Andantino **Strauss:** Allerseelen **Tchaikovsky:** Kamarinskaya
Myron Bloom, Cleveland Symphony

Intermediate Level
MMO CD 3513/8043
Massenet: Prelude **Mozart:** Concerto No. 4 (Romanza) **Rachmaninoff:** Vocalise **Scriabin:** Romance
Dale Clevenger, Cleveland Symphony

Intermediate Level
MMO CD 3514/8044
Beethoven: Adromeda **Francaix:** Canon in Octave **Mozart:** Quintet (Andante and Rondo)
Mason Jones, Philadelphia Orch.

Advanced Level
MMO CD 3515/8045
Beethoven: Sonata (Rondo) **Gliere:** Intermezzo **Mozart:** Concerto No. 2 (Andante and Rondo)
Myron Bloom, Cleveland Symphony

Advanced Level
MMO CD 3516/8046
Hindemith: Sonate (1st mvt.) **Mozart:** Concerto No. 4 (Rondo) **Strauss:** Concerto, Op. 11
Dale Clevenger, Cleveland Symphony

Intermediate Level
MMO CD 3517/8047
Handel: I See a Huntsman **Frackenpohl:** Allegro **Corelli:** Sonata in F (Prelude and Gavotte) **Mozart:** Concerto No. 3 (Romance)
Mason Jones, Philadelphia Orch.

Advanced Level
MMO CD 3518/8048
Hindemith: Sonate (2nd mvt.) **Mozart:** Concerto No. 1, 2nd mvt.(Allegro) **Schumann:** Adagio and Allegro
Myron Bloom, Cleveland Symphony

Intermediate Level
MMO CD 3519/8049
Corelli: Saraband and Gavotte **Mussorgsky:** A Tear **Saint-Saens:** Romance **Tchaikovsky:** Andante Cantabile
Dale Clevenger, Cleveland Symphony

Small numbers on far right indicate the cassette edition of each album **17**

Guitar

Boccherini: Guitar Quintet, No. 4 in D major, "Fandango"
MMO CD 3601/367
A consistent favorite of guitarists, yours to perform in your home.

Giuliani: Guitar Quintet Opus 65 in A Major
MMO CD 3602/368
Another favorite for the classical guitarist.

Classical Guitar Duets Easy-Medium
MMO CD 3603/4012
Lovely duets arranged by famed teacher, Leonid Bolotine. Andrew Lafreniere, soloist.
Chopin: Prelude 1 & 2; Etude **J.S.Bach:** Inventions, Menuet **Mozart:** Minuetto **Milan:** Pavan **Mendelssohn:** Spring Song **Bizet:** Pearl Fishers, Carcassi, Etude **Beethoven:** Minuet **Galilei:** Gagliarda **Offenbach:** Bacarolle, La Paloma, Romance Antiguo.

Renaissance & Baroque Guitar Duets
MMO CD 3604/5043
Anonymous: LaRossignol; Greensleeves; Drewries Accordes; My Lady Carey's Dompe; Lesson for Two Lutes **Johnson:** The Flatt Pavin; **Dowland:** Lord Chamberlain's Gailliard; Tarleton's Resurrection; Lord Willoughby's Welcome Home **Pilkington:** Echo **Le Sage de Richee:** Echo **J. S. Bach:** Musette; March; Polonaise; Menuet; Prelude; Fugue; Invention **Lawes:** Suite; Coront II **Telemann:** Canon.

Classical & Romantic Guitar Duets
MMO CD 3605/5044
Sor: Andantino, March, Duo in A **Carulli:** Study in A, Duo in E, Largo, Allegretto; Duet in F. Rondo (allegro) **Scheidler:** Romanze **Faure:** Sicilienne **Ackerman:** El Arroyo que Murmura **Granados:** Oriental Spanish Dance No.2 **Albeniz:** Malaguena

Guitar & Flute Duets, vol. 1
MMO CD 3606/5045
Anonymous: Greensleeves **Finger:** Division on a Ground **Faronell's:** Ground **E. G. Baron:** Sonata in G major **Dowland:** If My Complaints **Pilkington:** Rest Sweet Nymphs **J.S.Bach:** Sonata in D, BWV 1033 **Couperin:** Soeur Monique **Vivaldi:** Andante

Guitar & Flute Duets, vol. 2
MMO CD 3607/5046
Giuliani; Grand Sonata for Flute and Guitar **Faure:** Sicilienne **Ibert:** Entr'acte **Villa-Lobos:** Bachianas Brasileiras No.5, Distribution of the Flowers **Schubert:** An die musik.

Bluegrass Guitar
MMO CD 3608/185
Play along with "Country Cookin," as they romp through these bluegrass classics. Solos note-for-note in easy-to-follow tablature
Conceived and produced by Peter Wernick.
Dueling Banjos; The Ballad of Jed Clampett; Foggy Mountain Breakdown; Little Maggie; Lonesome Road Blues; All the Good Times are Past and Gone; Salty Dog Blues; Dark Hollow; Late Last Night; Jesse James; Roll on Buddy; Mountain Dew

Play the Guitar with George Barnes
MMO CD 3609/130
This best selling method by the legendary George Barnes contains a 52 lesson instruction book with accompanying CD. Learn chords, rhythms and various accompaniment styles including; ballads, blues, folk songs, country and western, shuffle rhythms and trick effects.

Play the Folk Guitar (2 CD Set)
MMO CD 3610/50
The most complete method of its kind ever published. Over 100 strums, 45 songs with chords and lyrics plus 70 photos. Learn Travis and Carter family style, bass runs, arpeggios, banjo style, blues, church lick, melody picking, solo and flat pick style.
Conceived by Dick Weissman and Dan Fox

Favorite Folk Songs
MMO CD 3611/160
Complete guitar parts, chords and lyrics to these classics, for you to sing-along or play-along!
He's Got the Whole World in His Hands; Silver Dagger; Hush Little Baby; Down in the Valley; East Virginia; Stackolee; Oh, Mary Don't You Weep; I Know Where I'm Going; Walking Boss; Spanish is the Loving Tongue; Man of Constant Sorrow; Banks of the Ohio; The Train; Sloop-John B; The Cukoo; Greensleeves; Key to the Highway; 500 Miles; Cool Colorado

For Guitars Only!
MMO CD 3612/4009
Jimmy Raney Small Band Arrangements
Spring is Here; Darn that Dream; How About You?; Just You, Just Me; Sunday; This Heart of Mine; Jupiter; I Got It Bad (And that Ain't Good); Fools Rush In; Beta Minus
Jack Wilkens, soloist

Ten Duets for Two Guitars MMO CD 3613/4011
Geo. Barnes/Carl Kress

Play The Blues Guitar
MMO CD 3614/140
Here are all the "blues" stylings for guitar, including Echo, Damping, Honky-tonk, Bottle-neck, Travis picking, Boogie Woogie, etc. An easy to follow method with 16 songs and loads of illustrations.
Frankie and Johnny; Careless Love; Step It Up and Go ; Kansas City Blues; Key to the Highway; Good Mornin' Blues; Red River; East St. Louis Blues; Railroad Bill • Stackolee; Ella Speed; St. James Infirmary; Betty and Duprée; Boogie Woogie; Every Night when the Sun Goes In; Blues in G ; My Momma Told Me

Orchestral Gems for Classical Guitar
MMO CD 3615
Tschaikovsky: Chanson Triste; **Korsakov:** Song Of India **Iradier:** La Paloma **Lehar:** Vilia **Bizet:** Adagietto (L'Arlesienne Suite) **Foster:** Old Folks At Home **Traditional:** Drink To Me Only With Thine Eyes **Gruber:** Silent Night **Offenbach:** Barcarolle
Andrew Lafreniere, soloist

Banjo

Bluegrass Banjo
MMO CD 4401/180
Solo to these classic banjo pieces, written out, note-for-note in easy to followtablature plus instruction in basic techniques for playing bluegrass music. Peter Wernick, noted Banjo Teacher is your instructor.
Dueling Banjos; The Ballad of Jed Clampett; Foggy Mountain Breakdown; Little Maggie; Lonesome Road Blues; All the Good Times are Past and Gone; Salty Dog Blues; Dark Hollow; Late Last Night; Jesses James; Roll on Buddy; Mountain Dew

Play The Five String Banjo Vol.1
by Dick Weissman
MMO CD 4402/186
A beginners method. Step-by-step instructions including: how to read music, chords, tuning, basic techniques, the Seeger strum, hammering on, etc.
Skip To My Lou; Go Tell Aunt Rhody; Polly Wolly Doodle; Hush Little Baby; Buffalo Gals; Whoa Mule; Red River Valley; Oh Susanna; London Bridge; Crawdad Song; Sourwood Mountain; Jesse James; Down In the Valley; Merrily We Roll Along; Wabash Cannonball; Clementine; Careless Love;Worried Man Blues

Play The Five String Banjo, Vol. 2
by Dick Weissman
MMO CD 4403/187
A banjo method. Step-by-step instruction including: Melody playing, more advanced hammering on and pulling off, an introduction to frailing and bluegrass styles, double thumbing, two and three finger picking, the pinch, etc.
Erie Canal; The Roving Gambler; Black Eyes Susie; The Boll Weevil; Darling Corey; Cripple Creek; Boatman Dance; She'll Be Comin' Round the Mountain; Old Dan Tucker; Goin' Down the Road; Feelin' Bad; When the Saints Go Marchin' In; Cumberland Gap; Little Margie

Drums

Bass

Modern Jazz Drumming (2 CD Set)   MMO CD 5001/4001

Jim Chapin's masterful study of today's drumming style, now in its 28th printing. The author has recorded and performed his famous studies in left hand independence. Listen, then play along with bassist Wilber Ware.

For Drummers Only!   MMO CD 5002/4002

An all-star band roaring through eight great standards, minus a drummer!Superbly planned and executed: a challenging set for every percussionist. Complete with 48-page book containing all the parts plus an analysis of modern drumming by Jim Chapin.

Wipe-Out   MMO CD 5003/4063

The most exciting titles in music built around the drum chair. Jim Chapin and Roger Pemberton have arranged these for an all-star aggregation including such players as Clark Terry, Hal McKusick, Hank Jones, George Duvivier, Harold Lieberman., Bob Wilber, Sonny Russo and YOU. Complete Drum Charts are provided.

Sit In   MMO CD 5004/4004

An all-star band consisting of Clark Terry, Jim Nottingham, Nick Travis, Frank Rehak, Sonny Russo, Bob Wilber, George Duvivier and Sonny Truitt provide superb Swing era, Dixie, Latin and Ballad backgrounds for you, including some sensational brass shouts. Preface, drum charts and general chatter by the dean of drum teachers, Jim Chapin.

Drum Star Jazz Combos   MMO CD 5005/4074

Join these trios, quartets and quintets in a superb set of jamming standards:

One Note Samba; Misty; Cool Jerk; I'll Remember April; Meditation and six more great standards.

Drumpadstickskin Jazz play-alongs   MMO CD 5006/4075

Provides the drummer with "club-date" experience. You get to perform with different sized combos, in Jazz, Latin, and Pop settings.

Terry's Tune; Watermelon Man; Song for My Father; Swingin' Shepherd's Blues; The Girl from Ipanema plus five more.

Classical Percussion (2 CD Set)   MMO CD 5009/4065

Arthur Press, former first chair percussionist of the Boston Symphony demonstrates many of the major orchestral drum solos and important themes for his instrument. The at-home player listens to either soloist or orchestra, which are on separate channels, in stereo. He can then play along with the full orchestra.This album is a "must" for the drummer whatever his aspirations. Mr. Press is one of the world's premier performers. He covers snare, bass drum, tambourine, triangle,castenets and cymbal technique in this tour of the classical repertoire.

8 Men In Search Of A Drummer   MMO CD 5010/4003

The John LaPorta Quintet and Octet play eight originals scored for drummers. Jam and trade 4^S and 8^S with the best. Chas. Perry charts.

Vibes

For Vibists Only!
A "Blues" Method   MMO CD 5101

A method for vibraphone prepared by famed Chicago vibist Shelly Elias. Built around blues, it suggests the many different styles for accompanying other instruments as well as soloing.

Good Vibe-rations
A "Pop" Method   MMO CD 5101

The role of vibraphonist in popular music. Includes examples of "comping' behind soloist as well as solo examples. Performed with full orchestra. You'll hear the author playing contemporary standards, than have your chance to follow suit at the vibraphone.

Laureate Series Contest Solos

Choice repertoire for the Double Bass selected and performed by David Walter, former department head at the Juilliard School of Music. Mr. Walter performs each piece, then practice them yourself. Annotated score provided plus written comments by the artist. In essence a Master Class.

Beginning to Intermediate Level   MMO CD 4301/8091/8094

J.S. Bach: Gavotte; Catalan Folk Song; The Bird ; Irish Folk Song; My Gentle Harp **Turetzky:** Bransle Simple, Fast Dance, Gavotte, Minuet **Tuthill:** Allegretto and Dorian Minuet **Walter:** Happy Blues, Israeli Dance, Japanese Lullaby; Russian March **Capuzzi:** Concerto (1st/2nd mvts.) **Saint-Saens:** The Elephant

Intermediate to Advanced Level   MMO CD 4302/8094/8097

Vivaldi: Sonata No.4 in Bb (1st/2nd mvts.) **Weinstein:** Modal Solos (Mixolydian and Hungarian) **Bottesini:** Concerto; Reverie **Dragonetti:** Concerto in A (1st mvt.) **Hindemith:** Sonata (1st mvt.)

Kenny Smith, bass virtuoso, produced the two marvelous albums that follow. They present the bassist with jazz situations encountered when performing in live club situations. The music, a mix of ballads, up-tempo songs and Latin rhythms is a joy to hear and play. Each program is well over an hour in length.

For Bassists Only!
Jazz Trios, Quartets, Quintets   MMO CD 4303/4072

One Note Samba; Misty; Feelin' Alright; Getting It Together; Oye Como Va; Psychedelic Sally; I'll Remember April; Meditation   *arranged and performed by Kenny Smith*

The Beat Goes On
Jazz Trios, Quartets, Quintets   MMO CD 4304/4073

Terry's Tune; Watermelon Man; Song for My Father; The Beat Goes On; John Brown's Body; Comin' Home Baby; The Girl from Ipanema   *arranged and performed by Kenny Smith*

From Dixie to Swing   MMO CD 4305

An all-star band led by pianist Dick Wellstood, joined by "Doc" Cheatham, trumpet; Vic Dickenson, trombone; Kenny Davern, poll winning clarinet and soprano sax; George Duvivier, bass and Gus Johnson, Jr., drums

Way Down Yonder in New Orleans; Sunny Side of the Street; Second Hand Rose; Exactly Like You; Rose of Washington Square; I Want a Little Girl; Red Sails in the Sunset; The Royal Garden Blues

Small numbers on far right indicate the cassette edition of each album   19

Vocal

In a field which is dominated by the vocal soloist, John Wustman is one of the few accompanists in this country who has achieved renown and critical acclaim in this most challenging of art forms. Mr. Wustman has developed that rare quality of bringing a strength and character to his accompaniments which create a true collaboration between the singer and the pianist. And this is as it should be, for in the art song especially, the piano part is not mere rhythmic and tonal background, but an integral part of the composer's intent and creation. Thus, on these records, Mr. Wustman provides not only the necessary accompaniment but also through his artistry, stylistic and interpretive suggestion for the study of the music.

Among the many artists he has accompanied in past years are: Gianna d'Angelo, Irina Arkhipova, Montserrat Caballe, Regine Crespin, Nicolai Gedda, Evelyn Lear, Mildred Miller, Anna Moffo, Birgit Nilsson, Jan Peerce, Roberta Peters, Elisabeth Schwarzkopf, Renata Scotto, Cesare Siepi, Giulietta Simionato, Thoms Stewart, Cesare Valetti and William Warfield.

Mr. Wustman has become known to millions of television viewers as the accompanist to Luciano Pavarotti in his many appearances in that medium.

> **"** *I have just heard my first MMO CD and was impressed with the musical artistry. My friends and I enjoy singing lieder and arias* **"**
> Shigeru K.
> Hitachiota, Japan

Schubert Lieder High Voice
MMO CD 4001/7001
An Die Musik; Die Forelle; Auf Dem Wasser Zu Singen; Du Bist Die Ruh; Wohin?; Nach Und Taume; Standchen; Heidenroslein; Gretchen and Spinnrade; Der Musensohn; Romanze Aus "Rosamunde"; Lachen Und Weinen; Der Tod Und Das Madchen; An Silvia; Seligkeit

Schubert Lieder Low Voice
MMO CD 4002/7002
An Die Musik; Auf Dem Wasser Zu Singen; Du Bist Die Ruh; Wohin?; Nach Und Taume; Standchen; Heidenroslein; Gretchen and Spinnrade; Der Musensohn; Romanze Aus "Rosamunde"; Der Tod Und Das Madchen; An Silvia; Seligkeit; Erikonig

Schubert Lieder High Voice Vol. 2   MMO CD 4003/7003
Fruhlingsglaube; Dass Sie Hier Gewesen; Im Fruhling; Die Liee Hat Gelogen; Du Liebst Mich Nicht; Erster Verlust; Die Allmacht; Ganymed; Wanderers Nachtlied; Nahe Des Geliebten; Fischerweise; Nachtviolen; Rastlose Liebe; Im Abendrot; Ungeduld

Schubert Lieder Low Voice Vol. 2   MMO CD 4004/7004
Fruhlingsglaube; Dass Sie Hier Gewesen; Im Fruhling; Die Liee Hat Gelogen; Du Liebst Mich Nicht; Erster Verlust; Die Allmacht; Ganymed; Wanderers Nachtlied/; Nahe Des Geliebten; Fischerweise; Nachtviolen; Rastlose Liebe; Im Abendrot; Ungeduld

Brahms Lieder High Voice   MMO CD 4005/7005
Liebestreu; Der Tod, Das Ist Die Kuhle Nacht; Wie Melodien Zieht Es Mir; Immer Leiser Wird Mein Schlummer; Standchen; Botschaft; O Wusst Ich Doch Den Weg Zuruck; Dein Blaues Auge; An Die Nachtigall; Bie Dir Sind Meine Gedanken; Von Ewiger Liebe; Die Mainacht; Sonntag; Vergebliches Standchen; Meine Liebe Ist Grun

Brahms Lieder Low Voice   MMO CD 4006/7006
Liebestreu; Sapphische Ode; Wie Melodien Zieht Es Mir; Immer Leiser Wird Mein Schlummer; Standchen; Botschaft; O Wusst Ich Doch Den Weg Zuruck; Dein Blaues Auge; An Die Nachtigall; Von Ewiger Liebe; Die Mainacht; Sonntag; Vergebliches Standchen; Meine Liebe Ist Grun; Auf dem Kirchofe

Everybody's Favorite Songs High Voice   MMO CD 4007/7007
Bach: My Heart Ever Faithful **Gounod:** Ave Maria **Schubert:** Ave Maria **Brahms:** Wiegenlied **Franz:** Dedication **Dvorak:** Songs My Mother Taught Me **Tchaikovsky:** None but the Lonely Heart **Grieg:** I Love Thee **Hahn:** Si Mes Vers Avaient Des Ailes **Faure:** Apres Un Reve **Moore:** Last Rose of Summer **Johnson:** Drink to Me Only with Thine Eyes **Quilter:** Now Sleeps the Crimson Petal **Haydn:** My Mother Bids Me Bind My Hair

Everybody's Favorite Songs Low Voice   MMO CD 4008/7008
Bach: My Heart Ever Faithful **Gounod:** Ave Maria **Schubert:** Ave Maria **Brahms:** Wiegenlied **Franz:** Dedication **Dvorak:** Songs My Mother Taught Me **Tchaikovsky:** None But the Lonely Heart **Grieg:** I Love Thee **Hahn:** Si Mes Vers Avaient Des Ailes **Faure:** Apres Un Reve **Moore:** Last Rose of Summer **Johnson:** Drink to Me Only With Thine Eyes **Quilter:** Now Sleeps the Crimson Petal **Haydn:** My Mother Bids Me Bind My Hair

Everybody's Favorite Songs High Voice Volume 2   MMO CD 4009/7009
Purcell: Music for a While **Torelli:** Tu Lo Sai **Mozart:** Das Veilchen **Handel:** Where'er You Walk **Beethoven:** Ich Liebe Dich **Schumann:** Der Nussbaum, Die Lotasblume **Schubert:** Litanei **Mendelssohn:** On Wings of Song **Bohm:** Still Wie Die Nacht **Traditional:** Londonderry Air, Greensleeves **Moore:** Believe Me, If All Those Endearing Young Charms **Debussy:** Beau Soir **Wolf:** Verborgenheit **Strauss:** Zueignung

Everybody's Favorite Songs Low Voice Vol. 2   MMO CD 4010/7010
Purcell: Music for a While **Torelli:** Tu Lo Sai **Mozart:** Das Veilchen **Handel:** Where'er You Walk **Beethoven:** Ich Liebe Dich **Schumann:** Der Nussbaum, Die Lotasblume **Schubert:** Litanei **Mendelssohn:** On Wings of Song **Bohm:** Still Wie Die Nacht **Traditional:** Londonderry Air, Greensleeves **Moore:** Believe Me, If All Those Endearing Young Charms **Debussy:** Beau Soir **Wolf:** Verborgenheit **Strauss:** Zueignung

17th/18th Century Italian Songs
High Voice   **MMO CD 4011**/7011

Caldara: Selve Amiche **Carissimi:** Vittoria, Mio Cuore **Monteverdi:** Lasciatemi Morire **Scarlatti:** Gia Il Sole Dal Gange **Caccini:** Udite, Amanti, Belle Rose Purpurine, Sfogava Conle Stelle **Cavalli:** Sospiri di Fuoco **Falconieri:** Bella Porta Di Rubini **Durante:** Vergin, Tutto Amor **Giordani:** Caro Mio Ben **Peri:** Nel Puro Ardor **Scarlatti:** Sento Nel Core

17th/18th Century Italian Songs
Low Voice   **MMO CD 4012**/7012

Caldara: Selve Amiche **Carissimi:** Vittoria, Mio Cuore **Monteverdi:** Lasciatemi Morire **Scarlatti:** Gia Il Sole Dal Gange **Caccini:** Udite, Amanti, Belle Rose Purpurine, Sfogava Conle Stelle **Cavalli:** Sospiri di Fuoco **Falconieri:** Bella Porta di Rubini **Durante:** Vergin, Tutto Amor **Giordani:** Caro Mio Ben **Peri:** Nel Puro Ardor **Scarlatti:** Sento Nel Core

17th/18th Century Italian Songs
High Voice Vol.2   **MMO CD 4013**/7013

Caccini: Amarilli **Legrenzi:** Che Fiero Costume **Durante:** Danza, Danza Fanciulla **Caccini:** Occhi Immortali **Cavalli:** Son Ancor Pargoletta **Scarlatti:** O Cessate di Piagarmi, Toglietemi La Vita Ancor **Staradella:** Se Nel Ben Sempre **Falconieri:** Occhietti Amati **Rontani:** Caldi Sospiri **Monteverdi:** Illustratevi, O Cieli **Rosa:** Vado Ben Spesso Cangiando Loco **Peri:** Gioite al Canto Mio

17th/18th Century Italian Songs
Low Voice Vol. 2   **MMO CD 4014**/7014

Caccini: Amarilli **Legrenzi:** Che Fiero Costume **Durante:** Danza, Danza Fanciulla **Caccini:** Occhi Immortali **Cavalli:** Son Ancor Pargoletta **Scarlatti:** O Cessate di Piagarmi, Toglietemi La Vita Ancor **Staradella:** Se Nel Ben Sempre; **Falconieri:** Occhietti Amati; **Rontani:** Caldi Sospiri **Monteverdi:** Illustratevi, O Cieli **Rosa:** Vado Ben Spesso Cangiando Loco **Peri:** Gioite Al Canto Mio

Famous Soprano Arias   **MMO CD 4015**/7015

Mozart: The Magic Flute -Ach, Ich Fuhl's; The Marriage of Figaro -Deh Vieni, Non Tardar **Puccini:** La Boheme - Mi Chiamano Mimi, Quando M'en Vo; Madama Butterfly - Un Bel Di Vedremo; La Traviata - Addio, Del Passato; Otello - Ave Maria **Verdi:** Falstaff - Sul Fil D'un Soffio Etesio **Weber:** Freischutz - Und Ob Die Wolke **Puccini:** Gianni Schicchi - O Mio Babbino Caro **Charpentier:** Louise -Depuis le Jour **Massenet:** Manon - Adieu, Notre Petite Table **Gounod:** Faust - Jewel Song

Famous Mezzo-Soprano Arias
    MMO CD 4016/7016

Gluck: Orfeo - Che Faro Senza Euridice **Handel:** Xerxes - Largo **Mozart:** Marriage of Figaro -Voi Che Sapete, Non So Piu Cosa Son **Thomas:** Mignon - Connais Tu Le Pays? **Ponchielli:** La Giocaonda -Voce di Donna **Verdi:** Il Trovatore -Stride La Vampa **Saint-Saens:** Samson et Dalila - Printemps Qui Commence, Amour, Viens Aider; Mon Coeur S'ouvre A Ta Vo **Bizet:** Carmen - Habanera, Seguidilla

Famous Tenor Arias   **MMO CD 4017**/7017

Mozart: The Magic Flute - Dies Bildnis; Don Giovanni - Dalla Sua Pace **Verdi:** La Traviata -De' Miei Bollenti Spiriti; Rigoletto - La Donna E Mobile; Lalo: Le Roi D'ys - Aubade **Gounod:** Faust - Salut! Demeure Chaste et Pure **Massenet:** Manon - Le Reve **Flotow:** Martha - M'appari; **Giordano:** Fedora - Amor Ti Vieta **Puccini:** Manon Lescaut - Donna Non Vidi Mai; Tosca - E Lucevan Le Stelle; La Boheme - Che Gelida Manina **Bizet:** Carmen - Flower Song

Famous Baritone Arias   **MMO CD 4018**/7018

Mozart: The Marriage of Figaro - Non Piu Andrai; Don Giovanni - Deh Vieni Alla Finestra; The Magic Flute - Der Vogelfanger Bin Ich Ja **Gounod:** Faust - Avant de Quitter Ces Lieux (Eb)(Db); **Verdi:** Il Trovatore -Il Balen Del Suo Soriso; La Traviato - Di Provenza Il Mar; Un Ballo In Maschera - Alla Vita Che T'arride, Eir Tu Che Macchiavi **Bizet:** Carmen - Toreador Song **Leoncavallo:** I Pagliacci - Prologue **Massenet:** Herodiade - Vision Fugitive **Wagner:** Tannhauser - O Du Mein Holder Abendstern

Famous Bass Arias   **MMO CD 4019**/7019

Mozart: The Magic Flute - O Isis Und Osiris, In Diesen Heil'gen Hallen; The Marriage of Figaro - Non Piu Andrai;**Gounod:** Faust - Vous Qui Faites L'endormie (Serenade), Le Veau D'or **Puccini:** La Boheme - Vecchia Zimmara **Verdi:** Falstaff - Quand'ero Paggio **Rossini:** The Barber of Seville - La Calunnia **Bellini:** La Sonnambula - Vi Ravviso, O Luoghi Ameni **Verdi:** Ernani - Infelice! E Tuo Cedevi; Don Carlo - Ella Giammai Mamo; Simone Boccanegra - Il Lacerto Spirito

Hugo Wolf Lieder
High Voice   **MMO CD 4020**/7071

Im Fruhling; Auf Ein Altes Bild; Gebet; Lebe Wohl; In Der Fruhe; Begegnung; Der Gartner; Schlafendes Jesuskind; Nun Lass Uns Frieden Schliessen; Verschwiegene Liebe; Nachtzauber; Herr, Was Tragt Der Boden Hier; Ach, Des Knaben Augen; Anakreons Grab; Epiphanias

Hugo Wolf Lieder
Low Voice   **MMO CD 4021**/7072

Im Fruhling; Auf Ein Altes Bild; Gebet; Lebe Wohl; In Der Fruhe; Auf Einer Wanderung; Der Gartner; Schlafendes Jesuskind; Um Mitternacht; Verschwiegene Liebe; Nachtzauber; Herr, Was Tragt Der Boden Hier; Ach, Des Knaben Augen; Nun Lass Uns Frieden Schliessen; Anakreons Grab

Richard Strauss Lieder
High Voice   **MMO CD 4022**/7073

Heimliche Afforderung; Allerseelen; Heimkehr; Nacht; Morgan; Wie Sollten Wir Geheim; Wiegenlied; Befreit; Waldseligkeit; Freundliche Vision; Mein Auge; Traum Durch Die Dammerung; Standchen; Ich Schwebe; Cacilie

Richard Strauss
Low Voice   **MMO CD 4023**/7074

Heimliche Afforderung; Allerseelen; Hoimkehr; Nacht; Morgan; Wie Sollten Wir Geheim; Du Meines Herzens Krohelen; Befreit; Waldseligkeit; Freundliche Vision; Ich Trage Meine Minne; Traum Durch Die Dammerung; Standchen; Ich Schwebe; Cacilie

Robert Schumann Lieder
High Voice   **MMO CD 4024**/7101

Ruckert - Widmung; Heine - Du Bist Wie Eine Blume; Eichendorff - In De Fremde; Eichendorff - Waldesgesprach, Mondnacht, Fruhlingsnach; Ruckert - Der Himmel Hat Eine Trane Geweint; Heine - Dein Angesicht; Kerner - Stille Tranen; Heine - Ich Grolle Nicht; Altkatholisches Gedicht - Requiem; Lenau - Meine Rose; Heine - Mit Myrten Und Rosen; Ruckert - Mein Schoner Stern; Heine - Schone Wiege Meiner Leiden

Robert Schumann Lieder
Low Voice   **MMO CD 4025**/7102

Ruckert - Widmung; Heine - Du Bist Wie Eine Blume; Eichendorff - In De Fremde, Waldesgesprach, Mondnacht, Fruhlingsnach; Ruckert - Der Himmel Hat Eine Trane Geweint; Heine - Dein Angesicht; Kerner - Stille Tranen; Heine - Ich Grolle Nicht; Byron - Aus Den Hebraischen Gesangen; Lenau - Meine Rose; Heine - Mit Myrten Und Rosen; Ruckert - Mein Schoner Stern!; Heine - Schone Wiege Meiner Leiden

Mozart Arias Soprano   **MMO CD 4026**/7103

Cosi Fan Tutte - Come Scoglio; Don Giovanni - Non Mi Dir; Le Nozze di Figaro - Porgi, Amor, Qualche Ris, Dove Sono; Cosi Fan Tutte' - In Vomini, Una Donna A Quindici Anni; Don Giovanni - Batti,Batti, O Bel Masetto; Verdrai, Carino , Se Sei Buono; The Abduction from the Seraglio-Ach,Ich Liebt

Verdi Arias Soprano   **MMO CD 4027**/7104

La Forza Del Destino - Pace,Pace,Mio Dio; Ernani -Ernani, In Volami; Un Ballo in Maschera -Morro, Mi Prima In Graz; Il Trovatore' - D'amor Sull' Ali Rosee; Don Carlo -Tu Che Le Vanita; Aida - Oh Patria Mie; Macbeth - Sleepwalking Scene - Una Maccia

Italian Arias Soprano   **MMO CD 4028**/7105

Handel: Julius Caesar - Vadoro Pupille, Piangero **Rossini:** William Tell -Selva Opaca **Puccini:** La Boheme - Donde Lieta Usci **Mascagni:** Cavalleria Rusticana -Voi Lo Sapete; **Cilea:** Adriana Lecouvreur -Io Son L'umile Ancella, Poveri Fiori **Catalani:** La Wally - Ebben, N'andro Lontana; Boito: Mefistofele - L'altra Notte **Ponchielli:** La Gioconda -Suicidio

French Arias Soprano   **MMO CD 4029**/7106

Gluck: Alceste - Divinites Du Styx; Iphigenie En Tauride - O Malheureuse Iphigeni **Massenet:** Le Cid - Pleurez! Pleurez, Mes Yeux! **Debussy:** L'enfant Prodigue - Recitative and Lia's Aria; Bizet: Carmen - Je Dis Que Rien Ne M'epouvante **Massenet:** Herodiade - Il est Doux, Il Est Bon **Gounod:** Faust - The King of Thule; Sapho - O Ma Lyre Immortelle

Soprano Oratorio Arias   **MMO CD 4030**/7075

Mozart: Alleluia, Et Incarnatus Est **Haydn:** On Mighty Wings, With Verdure Clad **Mendelssohn:** Hear Ye Israel! **Bach:** Ich Will Dir Mein Herze Schenken, Blute Nur **Handel:** Rejoice, Rejoice Greatly, Come Unto Him, I Know That My Redeemer Liveth

Alto Oratorio Arias   **MMO CD 4031**/7076

Handel: O Thou That Tellest Good Tidings To Zion, He Shall Feed His Flock, Thou Shall Bring Them In, In The Battle **Bach:** Prepare Thyself, Zion, Keep, O My Spirit, Buss' Und Reu', Erbarme Dich **Mendelssohn:** Prepare Thyself, ZionBut the Lord is Mindful; O Rest In The Lord

Tenor Oratorio Arias   **MMO CD 4032**/7078

Handel: Comfort Ye, Every Valley, Thou Shall Break Them, Waft Her, Angels; In Native Worth; Sound An Alarm! **Bach:** Deposuit **Mendelssohn:** If With All Your Hearts **Mendelssohn:** Then Shall The Righteous **Verdi:** Ingemisco

Bass Oratorio Arias   **MMO CD 4033**/7079

Haydn: Now Shines The Greatest Glory Of Heaven **Handel:** But Who May Abide The Day Of His Coming, The Trumpet Shall Sound, Why Do The Nations, Honor And Arms, Arm, Arm, Ye Brave!; **Mendelssohn:** Lord God Of Abraham, Is Not His Word Like Fire?, It Is Enough **Verdi:** Confutatis

Small numbers on far right indicate the cassette edition of each album

Vocal

Laureate Series Contest Solos

These editions feature recitals by established artists and accompaniments by fine pianists. Learn the songs by listening to the professional, then try them yourself. Selections are from the very best solo literature for the voice.

Beginning Soprano Solos Kate Hurney   **MMO CD 4041/9001**
Bononcini: Per la gloria d'adorarvi **Haydn:** My Mother Bids Me Bind My Hair;Old Melody: When Love Is Kind **Pergolesi:** Stizzoso, mio stizzoso **Purcell:** Man Is For the Woman Made **Sullivan:** The Moon And I **Weckerlin:** Bergere Legere and Jeune Fillette

Intermediate Soprano Solos Kate Hurney
             MMO CD 4042/9004
J.S. Bach: My Heart Ever Faithful **Brahms:** Vergebliches Standchen; **Duke:** Loveliest of Trees **Franck:** Panis Angelicus **Hahn:** Si mes vers avaient des aides **Mozart:** Das Veilchen **Paisiello:** Nel cor pin non mi sento **Puccini:** O Mio Babbino Caro

Beginning Mezz. Sop. Solos Fay Kittelson
             MMO CD 4043/9011
Barber: The Daisies **Beethoven:** Ich Liebe Dich **Campion:** Never Weather-Beaten Sail **Godard:** Chanson de Florian; **Hopkinson:** My Love is Gone to Sea **Niles:** I Wonder as I Wander **Pergolesi:** Se tu M'ami, Se Sospiri **Scarlatti:** O Cessate di Piagarmi **Schubert:** Haiden-Roslein **Thompson:** Velvet Shoes

Intermediate Mezz. Sop. Solos Fay Kittelson
             MMO CD 4044/9014
Brahms: Botschaft and der Tod, Das Ist die Kuhle Nacht **Handel:** Angels, Ever Bright and Fair **Ives:** Children's Hour and a Night Song **Lotti:** Pur di Cesti, O Bocca Bella **Massenet:** Elegie **Persichetti:** The Microbe **Scarlatti:** Le Violette

Advanced Mezz. Sop. Solos Fay Kittelson
             MMO CD 4045/9017
Bach: Esurientes Implevit Bongs **Caccini:** Amarillo Mia Bella **Chausson:** Les Papillons **Faure:** Adieu and Apres un Reve **Guion:** At the Cry of the First Bird **Purcell:** When I Am Laid In Earth **Wolf:** Fussreise

Beginning Contralto Solos Carline Ray   **MMO CD 4046/9021**
Brahms: Wiegenlied **Durante:** Vergin, Tutto Amor **Franz:** Es Had die Rose Sichbeklagt **MacGimsey:** Sweet Little Jesus Boy **Monteverdi:** Lasciatemi morire! **Mozart:** Die Ante **Scarlatti:** Se Florindo e Fedele **Spiritual:** Ride On, King Jesus!

Beginning Tenor Solos George Shirley   **MMO CD 4047/9031**
Handel: Ombra Mat Fu **McGill:** Duna **Purcell:** If Music Be the Food of Love **Scarlatti:** Cara, Cara e Dolce **Schubert:** Das Wandern **Shirley (arr.):** There is a Balm in Gilead

Intermediate Tenor Solos George Shirley   **MMO CD 4048/9034**
Dello Joio: There is a Lady Sweet and Kind **Leoncavallo:** Mattinata **Massenet:** Crepuscule **Mendelssohn:** Be Thou Faithful (Elijah) **Rachmaninoff:** In the Silence of Night **Swanson:** Night Song

Advanced Tenor Solos George Shirley
             MMO CD 4049/9037
Faure: Fleur Jette **Handel:** Every Valley (Messiah) **Scarlatti:** Sono Unite a Tormentarmi **Schubert:** Die Allmacht **Swanson:** Joy **Verdi:** Questra o Quella (Rigoletto)

Small numbers on far right indicate the cassette edition of each album

Pop songs

Great Standards   MMO CDG 105
I Left My Heart in San Francisco (Tony Bennett); Over the Rainbow (Judy Garland); Lover Man Oh Where Can You Be? (Linda Ronstadt); But Not for Me (Harry Connick); The Way He Makes Me Feel (Barbra Streisand); The Way We Were (Barbra Streisand); Night and Day (Frank Sinatra); New York, New York (Frank Sinatra)

Great Love Songs   MMO CDG 108
For All We Know (The Carpenters); Somewhere Out There (Ingram/Ronstadt); I Just Called to Say I Love You (Stevie Wonder); You Decorated My Life (Kenny Rogers); A Very Special Love Song (Charlie Rich); Through the Eyes of Love (Melissa Manchester); If (Bread); Stop in the Name of Love (The Supremes)

Hits of Frank Sinatra   MMO CDG 117
Come Fly with Me; I've Got You Under My Skin; Luck Be a Lady; Witchcraft; Love and Marriage; All of Me; (Love is) The Tender Trap; Fly Me to the Moon

Hits of Frank Sinatra   MMO CDG 1001
The Lady is a Tramp; I've Got You Under My Skin; Night and Day; I've Got the World on a String; Summer Wind; Witchcraft; Strangers in the Night; Chicago (That Toddling Town); My Way; New York, New York

Hits of Ray Charles   MMO CDG 1017
What'd I Say?; I Can't Stop Loving You; Georgia on My Mind; Born to Lose; Hallelujah, I Love Her So ; Unchain My Heart; America, the Beautiful; Cryin' Time; Busted; Hit the Road, Jack

Hits of Neil Diamond   MMO CDG 1018
Kentucky Woman; Forever in Blue Jeans; Girl, You'll be a Woman Soon; Cracklin' Rosie ; Sweet Caroline; Song Sung Blue ; You Don't Bring Me Flowers; Hello Again; Love on the Rocks; America

Hits of Sammy Davis Jr.   MMO CDG 1020
The Joker; Talk to the Animals; Who Can I Turn To; A Wonderful Day like Today; What Kind of Fool Am I; I've Gotta Be Me; That Old Black Magic; Too Close for Comfort; The Candy Man; Hey There

Hits of Tony Bennett   MMO CDG 1026
What Are You Afraid Of; The Good Life; A Taste of Honey; Maybe This Time; When Love Was All We Had; Here's That Rainy Day; I Left My Heart in San Francisco; When Joanna Loved Me; The Shadow of Your Smile; This is All I Ask

Hits of Tom Jones   MMO CDG 1028
It Looks Like I'll Never Fall in Love Again; I Believe; Without Love; Green, Green Grass of Home; Help Yourself • It's Not Unusual; Delilah; What's New, Pussycat; Love Me Tonight; She's a Lady

Hits of Bobby Darin and Frank Sinatra   MMO CDG 1029
Young at Heart; How Little We Know; For Once in My Life; Come Fly with Me; Nice 'N' Easy That's All; Clementine; Dream Lover; Beyond the Sea; Mack the Knife

Hits of Nat King Cole   MMO CDG 1032
Mona Lisa; Smile; Too Young; Unforgetable; A Blossom Fell; Somewhere Along the Way; Walkin' My Baby Back Home; Answer Me, My Love; Darling, Je Vous Aime Beaucoup; Pretend

Hits of Frank Sinatra Vol. 4   MMO CDG 1051
All of Me; Serenade in Blue; I'll Never Smile Again; Learnin' the Blues; (Love Is) The Tender Trap; The Song is You; They Can't Take that Away from Me; I'll Be Seeing You; All or Nothing at All; This Love of Mine

Hits of Engelbert Humperdink   MMO CDG 1065
Another Place, Another Time; Release Me (and Let Me Love Again); Winter World of Love; Am I That Easy to Forgets; Till • After the Lovin'; Spanish Eyes; A Man Without Love; Quando, Quando, Quando; The Way It Used to Be

Hits of Frank Sinatra Vol. 6   MMO CDG 1082
It's All Right with Me; You'd Be So Easy to Love; Here's to the Losers; Hey, Jealous Lover; Dream; All the Way; Pennies from Heaven; Close to You; Young at Heart; (Love Is) The Tender Trap

Hits of Tony Bennett   MMO CDG 1129
Nice Work if You Can Get It; Change Partners; One for My Baby (And One More for the Road); It Only Happens When I Dance with You; The Boulevard of Broken Dreams; Emily; Body and Soul; Speak Low; The Days of Wine and Roses; Steppin' Out with My Baby

Sinatra–In the Wee Small Hours   MMO CDG 1192
I See Your Face Before Me; I'll Never Be the Same; This Love of Mine; I Get Along Without You Very Well; Can't We Be Friends; When Your Lover Has Gone; In the Wee Small Hours; Dancing on the Ceiling; It Never Entered My Mind; I'll Be Around

Sing Sinatra with Strings   MMO CDG 1199
I Hadn't Anyone Till You; Night and Day; Misty; Stardust; Come Rain or Come Shine; It Might as Well Be Spring; Prisoner of Love; That's All; All or Nothing at All; Yesterday

Songs of George Gershwin   MMO CDG 1024
Oh, Lady Be Good; Embracable You; I've Got a Crush on You; Of Thee I Sing; Fascinatin' Rhythm; 'S Wonderful; How Long Has This Been Going On; But Not for Me; Someone to Watch Over Me; Bidin' My Time; The Man I Love; Somebody Loves Me

Songs of Cole Porter   MMO CDG 1025
Blow, Gabriel, Blow; You're the Top; Anything Goes; What is this Thing Called Love; Love for Sale; Let's Do It; I Get a Kick Out of You; Begin the Beguine; Just One of Those Things; You Do Something to Me; Night and Day

Lush Big Band Sounds   MMO CDG 1104
You're Driving Me Crazy; It's a Sin to Tell a Lie; You Make Me Feel so Young; Fools Rush In; Everywhere You Go; My Baby Just Cares for Me; Day In, Day Out; Near You; Darn that Dream; Little White Lies

Pop songs

"Many suppliers claim to have karaoke tapes and CD's but you quickly discover that they are nothing more than sing-alongs and not of the quality provided by your company."

Helen S.
New Brunswick, Canada

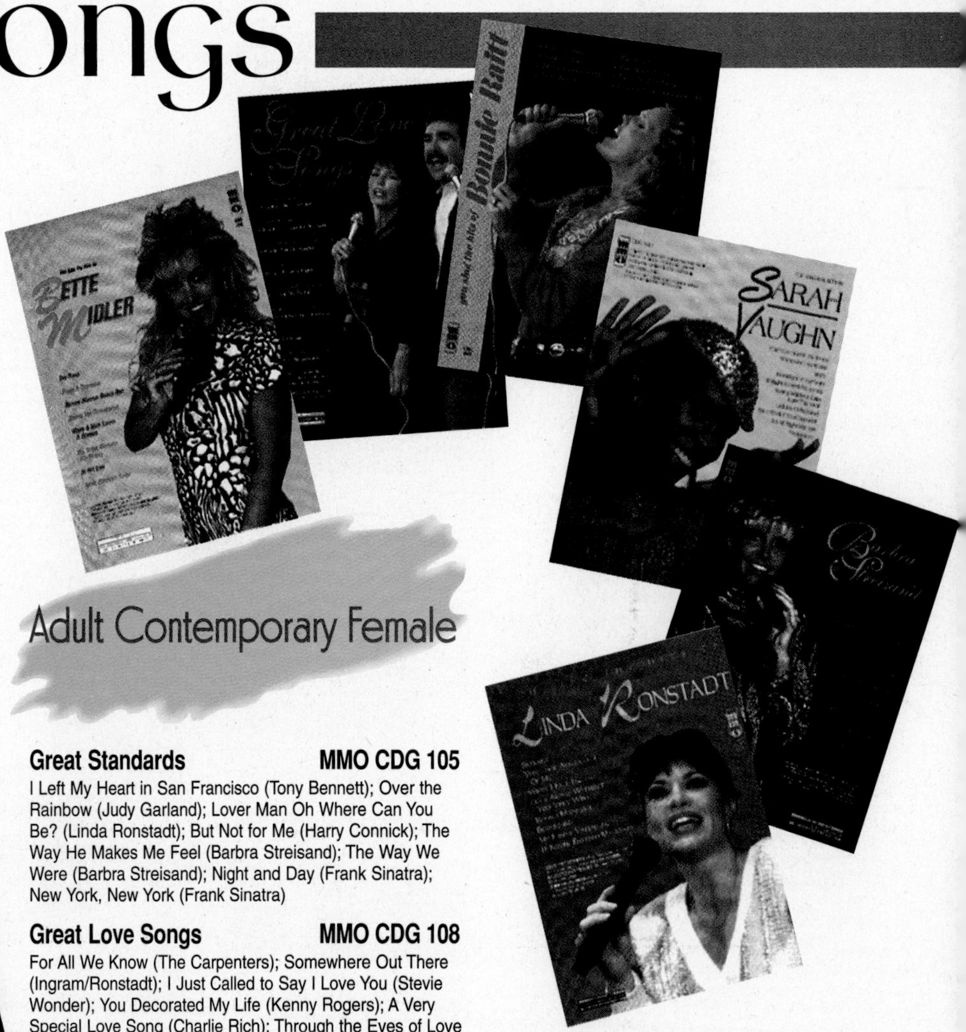

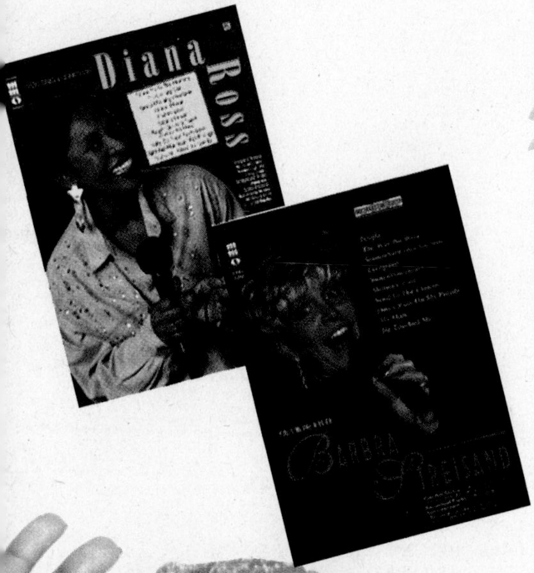

Adult Contemporary Female

Great Standards — **MMO CDG 105**
I Left My Heart in San Francisco (Tony Bennett); Over the Rainbow (Judy Garland); Lover Man Oh Where Can You Be? (Linda Ronstadt); But Not for Me (Harry Connick); The Way He Makes Me Feel (Barbra Streisand); The Way We Were (Barbra Streisand); Night and Day (Frank Sinatra); New York, New York (Frank Sinatra)

Great Love Songs — **MMO CDG 108**
For All We Know (The Carpenters); Somewhere Out There (Ingram/Ronstadt); I Just Called to Say I Love You (Stevie Wonder); You Decorated My Life (Kenny Rogers); A Very Special Love Song (Charlie Rich); Through the Eyes of Love (Melissa Manchester); If (Bread); Stop in the Name of Love (The Supremes)

Hits of Barbara Streisand — **MMO CDG 116**
As if We Never Said Goodbye; Luck Be a Lady; My Man; People ; Not While I'm Around; Send in the Clowns; Evergreen (A Star is Born); With One Look

Hits of Bette Midler — **MMO CDG 120**
Under the Boardwalk • From a Distance; The Rose; Boogie Woogie Bugle Boy; When a Man Loves a Woman; Wind Beneath My Wings; In My Life; Some People's Lives

Hits of Linda Ronstadt — **MMO CDG 123**
Skylark; You Took Advantage of Me; When I Fall in Love; I Get Along Without You Very Well; 'Round Midnight; Bewitched, Bothered and Bewildered; My Funny Valentine; It Never Entered My Mind

Hits of Barbra Streisand — **MMO CDG 1002**
He Touched Me; My Man; Don't Rain on My Parade; Send in the Clowns; Memory; Tomorrow (Annie); Evergreen; Somewhere; The Way We Were; People

Hits of Sarah Vaughan — **MMO CDG 1007**
Yesterdays; It's All Right With Me ; Nice Work if You Can Get It; Lullaby of Birdland; Spring Will be a Little Late This Year; It Might as Well Be Spring; Moonlight in Vermont; Misty; Whatever Lola Wants; Can't Get Out of this Mood

Hits of Linda Ronstadt — **MMO CDG 1012**
Bewitched, Bothered and Bewildered; When You Wish upon a Star; Sophisticated Lady; You Took Advantage of Me; Mean to Me; Skylark; When I Fall in Love; Lover Man (Oh Where Can You Be?); Crazy He Calls Me; What's New

Hits of Diana Ross — **MMO CDG 1027**
You're All I Need to Get By; Ain't No Mountain High Enough; Why Do Fools Fall in Love; Reach Out and Touch (Somebody's Hand); Upside Down; Endless Love; Mirror, Mirror; Good Morning Heartache; I'm Coming Out; Touch Me in the Morning

Hits of Bonnie Raitt — **MMO CDG 1052**
Have a Heart; Nick of Time; Thing Called Love; Love Letter; Runaway; Too Soon to Tell; Luck of the Draw; I Can't Make You Love Me

Hits of Celine Dion — **MMO CDG 1161**
Misled; When I Fall in Love; If You Asked Me To; Nothing Broken but My Heart; Love Can Move Mountains; The Power of Love; Where Does My Heart Beat Now?; The Colour of My Love

Hits of Bette Midler — **MMO CDG 1200**
In This Life; It's Too Late; I Believe in You ; I Know this Town; To Deserve You; The Perfect Kiss; Bottomless; To Comfort You; Bed of Roses; As Dreams Go By; The Last Time

Hits of Regina Belle — **MMO CDG 1202**
Could It Be I'm Falling in Love; Love T.K.O.; You Make Me Feel Brand New; Hurry Up This Way Again; The Whole Town's Laughing at Me; Didn't I (Blow Your Mind this Time); You are Everything; Let Me Make Love to You; Just Don't Want to be Lonely; I'll Be Around

HITS of Celine Dion — **MMO CDG 1220**
Because You Loved Me; Falling into You; I Love You; River Deep, Mountain High; If That's What it Takes; Seduces Me; Make You Happy; Call the Man

Small numbers on far right indicate the cassette edition of each album

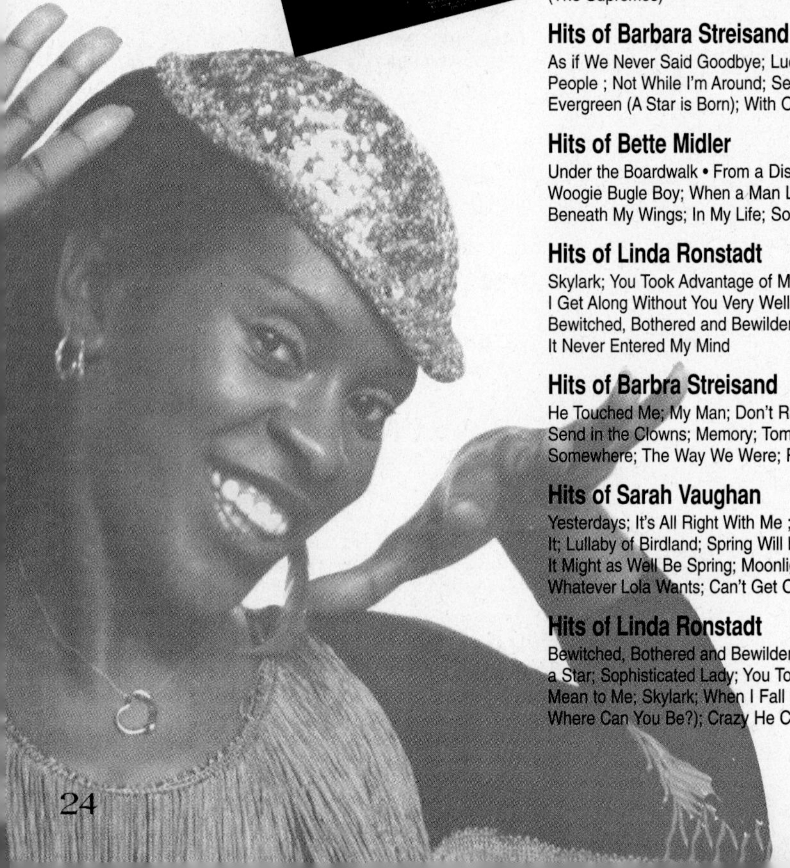

Rock/Pop Female

Pop Female Hits   MMO CDG 107
Dreamin' (Vanessa Williams); Same Ole Love (Anita Baker); Seasons Change; Expose a Deeper Love (Aretha Franklin); Breathe Again (Toni Braxton); Delta Dawn (Bette Midler); My Lovin' You're Never Gonna Get It (En Vogue); Blowing Kisses in the Wind (Paula Abdul)

Hits of the Carpenters   MMO CDG 114
Top of the World; We've Only Just Begun; Please Mr. Postman; I Won't Last a Day Without You; There's a Kind of Hush; Rainy Days and Mondays; Goodbye to Love; Yesterday Once More

Hits of Whitney Houston   MMO CDG 122
I Will Always Love You; The Greatest Love of All; Love Will Save the Day; All at Once; Didn't We Almost Have it All; I Wanna Dance with Somebody; Saving All My Love for You; Lover for Life

Female Chart Toppers   MMO CDG 132
Endless Love (M. Carey/L. Vandross); Lucky One (Amy Grant); I'll Remember (Madonna); Think Twice (Celine Dion); You Mean the World to Me (Toni Braxton); Love Sneakin' Up on You (Bonnie Raitt); Don't Turn Around (Ace of Base); The Sweetest Days (Vanessa Williams)

Pop Female Hits   MMO CDG 133
Turn the Beat Around (Gloria Estefan); Secret (Madonna); Body and Soul (Anita Baker); Without You (Mariah Carey); Stay (Lisa Loeb & Nine Stories); How Many Ways (Toni Braxton); You (Bonnie Raitt); Living in Danger (Ace of Base)

Hits of Whitney Houston   MMO CDG 1003
One Moment in Time; I Wanna Dance with Somebody (Who Loves Me); Didn't We Almost Have It All; All at Once; You Give Good Love; The Greatest Love of All; Saving All My Love for You

Hits of Janet Jackson   MMO CDG 1006
Alright; Escapade; Nasty; Miss You Much; Rhythm Nation; Control; Let's Wait Awhile; What Have You Done for Me Lately

Hits of the Carpenters   MMO CDG 1013
Hurting Each Other; (They Long to Be) Close to You; We've Only Just Begun; Top of the World; Rainy Days and Mondays; Sing; There's a Kind of Hush; I Won't Last a Day Without You; Goodbye to Love; Yesterday Once More

Debbie Gibson Hits   MMO CDG 1014
Electric Youth; No More Rhyme; Lost In Your Eyes; Staying Together; Foolish Beat; Out of the Blue; Shake You Love; Only in My Dreams

Hits of Paula Abdul   MMO CDG 1015
State of Attraction; Opposites Attract; Cold-Hearted; Straight Up; Next to You; (It's Just) The Way that You Love Me; Knocked Out; Forever Your Girl

Anita Baker Vol.1   MMO CD 1019
No One in the World; Caught Up in the Rapture; Sweet Love; Same Ole Love; Mystery; Been So Long; Just Because; Giving You the Best that I Got

Hits of Amy Grant   MMO CDG 1021
Angels; It's Not a Song; Sing Your Praise to the Lord; Father's Eyes; Love Will Find a Way; Thy Word; Lead Me On; Arms of Love; Wise Up

Hits of Sandi Patti   MMO CDG 1022
We Shall Behold Him; More Than Wonderful; How Majestic is Your Name; Via Dolorosa; Make His Praise Glorious; Shine Down; Lift up the Lord; Shepherd of My Heart

Hits of Madonna
MMO CDG 1035
Who's that Girl; Papa Don't Preach; Live to Tell; Cherish; Express Yourself; Oh, Father; Like a Virgin; Material Girl

Anita Baker Vol. 2   MMO CDG 1163
The Rhythm Of Love; Body and Soul; Soul Inspiration; Sweet Love; You Belong to Me; Sometime I; Wonder Why; The Look of Love; I Apologize

Hits of Annie Lennox   MMO CDG 1214
No More "I Love You's"; Why?; Here Comes the Rain Again; Train in Vain; Sweet Dreams are Made of This; A Whiter Shade of Pale; Little Bird; Walkin' On Broken Glass

Year of the Woman   MMO CDG 1215
Right Hand Man; You Oughta Know; Crazy Cool; You'll See; Carnival • Exhale (Shoop Shoop); You Got It; In This Life

Hits of Mariah Carey*   MMO CDG 1216
Can't Let Go; All I Ever Wanted; Emotions; I'll Be There; Music Box; You Need Me; Never Forget You; I Don't Wanna Cry
*Ms. Carey's publishers do not permit reprint of lyrics

Hits of Oleta Adams   MMO CDG 1217
Never Knew Love; I Knew You When; Slow Motion; We Will Meet Again; If This Love Should End; Life Keeps Moving On; Rhythm of Love; Get Here

Diana Ross Hits   MMO CDG 1218
Take Me Higher; Voice of the Heart; If You're Not Gonna Love Me Right; I Never Loved a Man Before; Gone; I Will Survive; Last Time I Saw Him; Ain't No Mountain High Enough

Selena in English & Spanish
    MMO CDG 1222
Amor Prohibito; Dondequiera Que Estes (Wherever You Are); Tu Solo Tu; El Toro Relajo; Como la Flor (Like a Flower); I Could Fall in Love; I'm Getting Used to You; Captive Heart; Dreaming of You

Hits of Gloria Estefan   MMO CD 1010
Anything For You*; Rhythm Is Gonna Get You*; Can't Stay Away From You*; Betcha Say That*; Conga*; Words Get In The Way*; Bad Boys; Don't Wanna Lose You; Here We Are*

Hits of Tina Turner   MMO CD 1060
What's Love Got to Do With it; Private Dancer; We Don't Need Another Hero; The Best; Typical Male; Two People; Let's Stay Together; River Deep, Mountain High*; Proud Mary

Female Hits of the 90's   MMO CD 1087
No Ordinary Love (Sade); I Will Always Love You (Whitney Houston); Love Is (McKnight/Williams); Love Can Move Mountains; (Celine Dion); Work To Do (Vanessa Williams; I See Your Smile* (Gloria Estefan); I'm Every Woman (Whitney Houston); Give It Up, Turn It Loose (En Vogue)

Hot Chart Hits for Women   MMO CD 1097
Saving Forever for You (Shanice); Save the Best for Last (Vanessa Williams); Deeper and Deeper (Madonna); Real Love (Mary J. Blige); Sometimes Love Just Ain't Enough (Patty Smyth); I'll Be There (Mariah Carey); Weak (SWV); That's the Way Love Goes (Janet Jackson)

Hits of Mariah Carey   MMO CD 1132
Dreamlover*; Hero*; Anytime You Need a Friend*; Just to Hold You Once Again*; Without You; Someday*; Love Takes Time*; Make It Happen*; Vision Of Love*

Hits of Mariah Carey   MMO CD 1205
Fantasy; Underneath the Stars; Melt Away; One Sweet Day; Forever; Open Arms; Always Be My Baby; When I Saw You; Long Ago

Hits of Roxette   MMO CD 3009
Dangerous; Dressed for Success; It Must Have Been Love; Joyride; The Look; Sleeping in My Car; Fading Like a Flower; Listen to Your Heart; Church of Your Heart

Please send your latest catalog of MMO-Pocket Songs. I find these recordings very useful to practice with and appreciate the quality you offer.

Celine Dion
Montreal, Canada

Pop songs

Rock/Pop Male

Pop Male Hits   MMO CDG 106
Come and Talk to Me (Jodeci); Blaze of Glory (Bon Jovi); Reach Out, I'll Be There (Michael Bolton); Alone with You (Tevin Campbell) • Addicted to Love (Robert Palmer); It's So Hard to Say Goodbye (Boyz II Men); How Am I Supposed to Live Without You (Michael Bolton); I'd Do Anything for Love (Meat Loaf)

Hits of Neil Diamond Vol.1   MMO CDG 113
Songs of Life; Shilo; Red, Red Wine; Forever in Blue Jeans; Desiree; Brother Love's; Traveling Salvation Show; America; September Morn

Hits of the Carpenters   MMO CDG 114
Top of the World; We've Only Just Begun; Please Mr. Postman; I Won't Last a Day Without You; There's a Kind of Hush; Rainy Days and Mondays; Goodbye to Love; Yesterday Once More

Hits of Elton John   MMO CDG 115
Candle in the Wind; Don't Let the Sun Go Down on Me; Goodbye Yellow Brick Road; Daniel; Crocodile Rock; Blue Eyes; Sacrifice; Rocket Man

Hits of Elvis Presley   MMO CDG 118
Blue Suede Shoes; Jailhouse Rock; Are You Lonesome Tonight; Blue Christmas; Suspicious Minds; Long Tall Sally; An American Trilogy; Crying in the Chapel

Hits of Neil Diamond Vol.2   MMO CDG 125
Girl, You'll be a Woman Soon; Hello Again; You Don't Bring Me Flowers; I Am, I Said; If You Know What I Mean; Kentucky Woman; Love on the Rocks

Male Chart Toppers   MMO CDG 130
People Get Ready (Rod Stewart); Objects in the Rearview (Meat Loaf); Completly (Michael Bolton); Endless Love (L. Vandross/M. Carey); But It's Alright (Huey Lewis); I Swear (All-4-One); You Let Your Heart Go Too Fast (Spin Doctors); You Better Wait (Steve Perry)

Pop Male Hits   MMO CDG 131
Hold My Hand (Hootie & Blowfish; Always (Bon Jovi); I'll Make Love to You (Boyz II Men); Shine (Collective Soul) • The Simple Things (Joe Cocker); You Don't Know How it Feels (Tom Petty); I'm Tore Down (Eric Clapton); Ain't Got Nothing (Michael Bolton).

Hits of Neil Diamond Vol.3   MMO CDG 137
Song Sung Blue; Cracklin' Rosie; Beautiful Noise; Cherry, Cherry; Holly Holly; Play Me; Soolaimon; Sweet Caroline

Hits of Elvis Presley   MMO CDG 1004
The Wonder of You; Can't Help Falling in Love; Stuck on You; It's Now or Never; Let Me Be Your Teddy Bear; One Night; Kentucky Rain; In the Ghetto; Moody Blue; If I Can Dream

Hits of Roy Orbison   MMO CDG 1008
It's Over; Dream Baby; Blue Bayou; Candy Man; Blue Angel; In Dreams; Crying; Running Scared; Only the Lonely; Oh, Pretty Woman

Hits of Billy Joel   MMO CDG 1011
Piano Man; It's Still Rock and Roll to Me; Only the Good Die Young; She's Always a Woman to Me; New York State of Mind; Tell Her About It • Just the Way You Are; We Didn't Start the Fire

Hits of the Carpenters   MMO CDG 1013
Hurting Each Other; (They Long to Be) Close to You; We've Only Just Begun; Top of the World; Rainy Days and Mondays; Sing; There's a Kind of Hush; I Won't Last a Day Without You; Goodbye to Love; Yesterday Once More

Hits of Phil Collins   MMO CD 1037
A Groovy Kind Of Love; One More Night; Easy Lover*; Against All Odds (Take A Look At Me Now)*; Take Me Home*; Separate Lives*; You Can't Hurry Love ; Sussudio*; In The Air Tonight'

Hits of Elvis Presley, Vol.2   MMO CD 1049
All Shook Up; Burning Love; Heartbreak Hotel; Are You Lonesome Tonight; Return To Sender; Jailhouse Rock; Hound Dog; Don't Be Cruel (To A Heart That's True); Blue Suede Shoes; Love Me Tender

Elvis Presley - The Sun Years   MMO CD 1057
That's All Right; Blue Moon Of Kentucky; Good Rockin' Tonight; I Love You Because; Just Because; Baby, Let's Play House; I Don't Care If The Sun Don't Shine; I'm Left, You're Right, She's Gone; Tomorrow Night; Harbor Lights

Hits of Richard Marx   MMO CD 1058
Satisfied; Right Here Waiting; Take this Heart Angelia; Don't Mean Nothing; Endless Summer Nights; Hazard; Hold on to the Nights

Hits of Queen   MMO CD 1059
Crazy Little Thing Called Love; Another One Bites the Dust; We Are the Champions; Radio Ga-Ga; The Show Must Go On; Bohemian Rhapsody • Kind Of Magic; The Miracle; I Want it All

Hits of Elton John   MMO CD 1061
Goodbye Yellow Brick Road ; Don't Let the Sun Go Down on Me; Candle in The Wind; Rocket Man; Blue Eyes; Sacrifice; Daniel; Nikita

Rock And Metal Ballads   MMO CD 1062
Wind Of Change (Scorpions); (Everything I Do) I Do It For You (Bryan Adams): Is This Love(Whitesnake): Don't Cry (Guns 'n' Roses): Carrie (Europe): Sweet Child O' Mine (Guns 'n' Roses): I Want To Know What Love Is (Foreigner): Right Here Waiting (Richard Marx)

Hits of Michael Jackson   MMO CDG 1063
Beat It; Billie Jean; Rock with You; Wanna Be Startin' Somethin'; Don't Stop till You Get Enough; Dirty Diana; Another Part of Me; Man in the Mirror; Bad

Hits of Rod Stewart   MMO CD 1064
Do Ya Think I'm Sexy; Maggie May; Tonight's The Night; Forever Young; You're Iin My Heart (the Final Acclaim); Downtown Train; My Heart Can't Tell You No; The Motown Song

Karaoke Party   MMO CD1071
Wind of Change (Scorpions); (Everything I Do) I Do It for You; (Bryan Adams); The Rose (Bette Midler); Rock Around the Clock; (Bill Haley & The Comets); Memory* (Barbra Streisand); Like a Virgin (Madonna); New York, New York (Frank Sinatra); One Moment in Time (Whitney Houston); What's Love Got to Do With It (Tina Turner)

Hits of James Taylor   MMO CDG 1072
Never Die Young; Sweet Potato Pie; Country Road; Up on the Roof; Like Everyone She Knows; Don't Let Me Be Lonely Tonight; How Sweet It Is (To Be Loved by You); Handyman; Fire and Rain; You've Got a Friend

Contemporary Rhythm & Blues   MMO CD 1073
Slow Dance-Hey Mr. DJ (R. Kelly/Public Announc); Alone With You (Tevin Campbell); Kickin' It (After 7); Can You Handle It?; (Gerald Levert); Money Can't Buy You Love (Ralph Tresvant); I've Been Searchin' (Glenn Jones); Honey Love (R Kelly/Public Announc); Goodbye (Tevin Campbell)

Elvis at the Movies   MMO CD 1074
Viva Las Vegas; Puppet On a String (Girl Happy); Separate Ways; Follow that Dream; Kissin' Cousins; Memories; Don't Cry Daddy; It's Over; Wear My Ring around Your Neck; Home is Where the Heart Is; Please Don't Stop Loving Me

Peabo Bryson & Bobby Brown   MMO CD 1081
A Whole New World*; Can You Stop the Rain;• If Ever You're in My Arms Again; Something in Common; I'm Your Friend; Every Little Step; My Prerogative; Beauty and the Beast*

Hits of Michael Bolton   MMO CD 1085
(Sittin' On) The Dock of the Bay; How am I Supposed to Live Without You; Soul Provider; You Send Me; Drift Away; Knock on Wood; Since I Fell For You; To Love Somebody; Reach Out, I'll Be There

D.J. Party   MMO CD 1088
Strokin' (Clarence Carter); Red, Red Wine (UB40); Jamming (Bob Marley); Together Forever (Rick Astley); Conga* (Miami Sound Machine); Electric Slide (Marcia Griffith); Celebration (Kool and the Gang); Limbo Rock (Chubby Checker); Shout! (Isley Brothers); Hot, Hot, Hot (Buster Poindexter)

Male Hits of the 90's   MMO CD 1096
The Crying Game (Boy George); Reach Out, I'll Be There (Michael Bolton); Do It To Me (Lionel Richie); Heal the World*; (Michael Jackson); The One (Elton John); Every Little Step (Bobby Brown); If Ever You're in My Arms Again (Peabo Bryson); Too Funky (George Michael); Just Another Day (Jon Secada)

Hits of Michael Bolton Vol.2   MMO CD 1107
Soul of My Soul; Said I Loved You...But I Lied; The One Thing; A Time for Letting Go; In the Arms of Love; Georgia on My Mind; When I'm Back on My Feet Again; How Can We Be Lovers

Hits of Reggae   MMO CD 1109
I Shot the Sheriff (Bob Marley); No Woman No Cry (Bob Marley); Could You Be Loved (Bob Marley); Three Little Birds (Bob Marley); Can't Help Falling In Love (UB40); The Way You Do The Things You Do (UB40); Look Who's Dancin' (Ziggy Marley); One Bright Day (Ziggy Marley)

D.J . Party Vol.2   MMO CD 1111
Y.M.C.A* (Village People); The Shoop Shoop Song-It's In His Kiss (Cher); Na Na Hey Hey-Kiss Him Goodbye (The Steam); Piano Man Billy Joel) ; The Time Warp (Rocky Horror Show); Get On Your Feet* (Gloria Estefan); Kokomo (The Beach Boys); Louie Louie (The Kingsmen); Pink cadillac*; (Natalie Cole); Hanky Panky (Tommy James & Shondells)

D.J. Party Vol. 3   MMO CDG 1112
Old Time Rock and Roll (Bob Seger); That's the Way I Like It; (KC and the Sunshine Band); Rock this Town (Stray Cats); I Love Rock 'N' Roll (Joan Jett); Last Dance (Donna Summer); We Didn't Start the Fire (Billy Joel); Smokin' in the Boys' Room (Motley Crue); Johnny B. Goode (Chuck Berry); Mony, Mony (Tommy James & Shondells); 1-2-3 (Miami Sound Machine)

D.J. Party Vol. 4   MMO CDG 1113
Born to Be Wild (Steppenwolf); Macho Man (Village People); Super Freak (Rick James); Bad to the Bone (George Thorogood); Bad Girls (Donna Summer); Short People (Randy Newman); Do Ya Think I'm Sexy (Rod Stewart); Caribbean Queen (Billy Ocean); The Monster Mash (Bobby Pickett)

Hits of Stevie Wonder   MMO CD 1120
Boogie on Reggae Woman; I Just Called to Say I Love You; Isn't She Lovely; Higher Ground; You and I; Sir Duke; For Once in My Life; Ribbon in the Sky; Superstition; Do I Do

Brill Building - Neil Diamond   MMO CD 1126
Do You Know The Way To San Jose; Don't Make Me Over; Don't Be Cruel (To a Heart That's True); You've Lost that Lovin' Feelin'; I (Who Have Nothing)*; A Groovy Kind of Love; Spanish Harlem*; Save the Last Dance for Me; Happy Birthday, Sweet Sixteen; Will You Still Love Me Tomorrow

Elton John Duets   MMO CD 1128
When I Think About Love; The Power; Shakey Ground; Don't Go Breaking My Heart; Don't Let the Sun Go Down on Me; Go On and On; Ain't Nothing Like the Real Thing; Love Letters

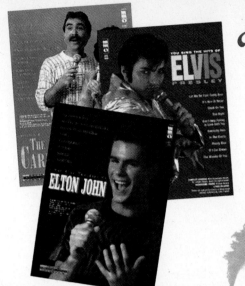

Hits of Bon Jovi   MMO CD 1152
Bed Of Roses; Blaze Of Glory; I'll Be There For You; Never Say Goodbye; Runaway; You Give Love a Bad Name; Silent Night; Bad Medicine

Elton John Duets   MMO CD 1165
The Power; Shakey Ground; If You Were Me; Don't Go Breaking My Heart; Don't Let the Sun Go Down on Me; Teardrops; Ain't Nothing Like the Real Thing; Love Letters

Hits of Sting   MMO CD 1166
If I Ever Lose My Faith in You; When We Dance; Nothing 'Bout Me; Fortress Around Your Heart; If You Love Somebody, Set Them Free; Be Still My Beating Heart; Love is the Seventh Wave; Russians; We'll Be Together

The Best of R & B Vol. 1   MMO CD 1190
Baby, I Need Your Loving (Four Tops); My Girl (Temptations); Under the Boardwalk (Drifters); Well-A-Wiggy (Weather Girls); What a Wonderful World* (Sam Cooke); Rainy Day Bells (Globetrotters); I Know I'm Losing You (Temptations); Another Saturday Night* (Sam Cooke); I Can't Help Myself (Four Tops); Up on the Roof (Drifters)

You Sing Hootie & the Blowfish   MMO CDG 1201
Hold My Hand; Running from an Angel; Hannah Jane; Let Her Cry; I'm Goin' Home; Only Wanna Be; With You; Not Even the Trees; Drowning; Goodbye

Boyz II Men   MMO CDG 1211
Visions of a Sunset; Water Runs Dry; Vibin'; On Bended Knee; I'll Make Love to You; One Sweet Day; In the Still of the Night; End of the Road

George Michael's Latest Hits   MMO CDG 1224
Jesus to a Child; Fastlove; Older; It Doesn't Really Matter; Star People; To Be Forgiven; Move On

Hits of Abba   MMO CD 3001
Fernando; Angel Eyes; Dancing Queen; Knowing Me Knowing You; Super Trouper; The Winner Takes it All; Waterloo; Take a Chance on Me

Hits of Joe Cocker   MMO CDG 3002
Unchain My Heart; The Letter; Cry Me a River; Up Where We Belong; The Simple Things; Have a Little Faith; Trust in Me; With a Little Help from My Friends

Hits of R.E.M.   MMO CD 3003
Everybody Hurts ; It's The End of the World as We Know It; Losing My Religion; The One I Love; Radio Free Europe; Shiny Happy People; Stand; What's the Frequency Kenneth

Hits of Phil Collins Vol. 2   MMO CD 3004
Another Day in Paradise; Do You Remember; Everyday; Find a Way To My Heart; I Wish it Would Rain; Only You Know and I Know; Something Happened on the Way to Heaven

Hits of Inxs   MMO CD 3005
Beautiful Girl; Devil Inside; Need You Tonight; Never Tear Us Apart; Suicide Blonde; New Sensation; Shining Star; What You Need

Hits Of Eric Clapton   MMO CD 3006
After Midnight; I Shot The Sheriff; Layla (MTV Unplugged); I'm Tore Down; Lay Down Sally; Motherless Child; Tears in Heaven; Hoochie Coochie Man

Hits of Bryan Adams   MMO CDG 3008
Can't Stop this Thing We Started; Do I Have to Say the Words; Please Forgive Me; Summer of '69; Thought I'd Died and Gone to Heaven; All for Love; (Everything I Do) I Do It for You

Hits Of The Rolling Stones   MMO CD 3010
Start Me Up; Harlem Shuffle; It's Only Rock And Roll; Love is Strong; You Got Me Rocking; Out of Tears; Satisfaction; Angie

Pop songs

Oldies Songs

Motown

Motown Memories (Male)   MMO CDG 1118
My Cherie Amour (Stevie Wonder); I Heard it Through the Grapevine (Marvin Gaye); Baby, I Need Your Loving (Four Tops); I Can't Help Myself (Four Tops); Being with You (Smokey Robinson); How Sweet It Is To *Be Loved by You* (Marvin Gaye); I'll Be There (Jackson Five); My Girl (Temptations); I Second that Emotion (Smokey Robinson); You are the Sunshine of My Life (Stevie Wonder)

Motown Memories (Female)   MMO CDG 1119
Stop in the Name of Love (The Supremes); Please Mr. Postman (Marvelettes); Love is Like a Heatwave (Martha & The Vandellas); My Guy (Mary Wells); Where Did Our Love Go (The Supremes); Baby Love (The Supremes); Dancing in the Street (Martha & The Vandellas); Ain't No Mountain High Enough (Diana Ross); If I Were Your Woman (Gladys Knight/Pips); Touch Me in the Morning (Diana Ross)

Gospel

HITS OF AMY GRANT
MMO CDG 1021
Angel; It's Not a Song; Sing Your Praise to the Lord; Father's Eyes; Love Will Find a Way; Thy Word; Lead Me On; Arms of Love; Wise Up

HITS OF SANDI PATTI
MMO CDG 1022
We Shall Behold Him; More than Wonderful; How Majestic is Your Name; Via Dolorosa; Make His Praise Glorious; Shine Down; Lift Up the Lord; Shepherd of My Heart

Hits of the 60's   MMO CDG 109
Me and Bobby McGee (Janis Joplin); I'm Henry the VIII, I Am (Herman's Hermits); Baby Love (The Supremes); You Must Have Been a Beautiful Baby (Bobby Darin); Tears of a Clown (Smokey Robinson); Danke Schoen (Wayne Newton); Spanish Eyes (Engelbert Humperdinck); Ebb Tide (Righteous Brothers)

Hits of the 50's   MMO CDG 110
Ain't That a Shame (Fats Domino); The Wonder of You (Elvis Presley); Save the Last Dance for Me (Drifters); On Broadway (Drifters); Love is Like a Heatwave (Martha & the Vandellas; Only the Lonely (Roy Orbison); Blue Moon (Marcels); My Boyfriend's Back (The Angels)

Hits of the 50's   MMO CDG 1030
He's So Fine; The Wanderer (Dion and the Belmonts); Runaround Sue (Dion and the Belmonts); Where the Boys Are (Connie Francis); Stop in the Name of Love (The Supremes); It's My Party (Leslie Gore); In the Still of the Night (The Five Satins); Earth Angel, Will You Be Mine? (The Penguins); Johnny B. Goode (Chuck Berry); Sixteen Candles (Johnny Maestro)

Hits of the 60's   MMO CDG 1031
Louie Louie (The Kingsmen); Down on Me (Janis Joplin); Monday, Monday (Mamas and the Papas); Under the Boardwalk (Drifters); Like a Rolling Stone (Bob Dylan); Good Lovin' (Rascals); Hit the Road, Jack (Ray Charles); Whole Lotta Shakin' Goin' On (Jerry Lee Lewis); Leaving on a Jet Plane (Peter Paul and Mary); Love is Just a Four Letter Word (Joan Baez)

Profile of the 80's   MMO CDG 1108
Lady (Kenny Rogers); Physical (Olivia Newton-John); Ebony and Ivory (McCartney/Wonder); Every Breath You Take (Police); Like a Virgin (Madonna); Say You, Say Me (Lionel Richie); One More Try (George Michael); Walk Like an Egyptian (The Bangles); Another Day in Paradise (Phil Collins)

Oldies Groups

The Coasters and the Drifters MMO CDG 127
Some Kind of Wonderful; Yakety Yak; Charlie Brown; Searchin'; Poison Ivy; There Goes My Baby; This Magic Moment; Up on the Roof

The Platters   MMO CDG 139
My Prayer; With this Ring; Washed Ashore; Only You (and You Alone); (You've Got) The Magic Touch; Smoke Gets in Your Eyes; The Great Pretender; Twilight Time

Hits of the Beatles   MMO CDG 1005
Penny Lane; Strawberry Fields Forever; Hey Jude; Norwegian Wood; The Fool on the Hill; Getting Better all the Time; Yesterday; Michelle; Let It Be; Eleanor Rigby

Female Groups of the 60's   MMO CDG 1036
Give Him a Great Big Kiss (Shangrilas); Lover's Concerto (Toys); My Boyfriend's Back (The Angels); Walking in the Rain (Ronettes); Uptown (Crystals); Leader of the Pack (Shangrilas); Will You Still Love Me Tomorrow (Shirelles); Our Day Will Come (Ruby and the Romantics); Summertime, Summertime (Jamies); Sunday Will Never be the Same (Spanky & Our Gang)

Male Groups of the 60's   MMO CDG 1038
A World Without Love (Peter and Gordon); Black and White (Three Dog Night); Daydream Believer (Monkees); Do Wah Diddy Diddy (Manfred Mann); Lady Willpower (Gary Puckett); Mr. Tambourine Man (Byrds); Only in America (Jay and the Americans); Sugar Shack (Jimmy Gilmer/Fireballs); The Letter (Box Tops); You've Lost That Lovin' Feelin' (Righteous Brothers)

Hits of the Beach Boys   MMO CDG 1039
Surfin' USA; Barbara Ann; I Get Around; Help Me Rhonda; Fun, Fun, Fun; Surfer Girl; Be True to Your School; California Girls; Sloop John B; Wouldn't It Be Nice

Rock and Roll Classics   MMO CDG 1066
Rock Around the Clock (B. Haley &The Comets); Tutti Frutti (Little Richard); Rock & Roll Music (C. Berry); Blue Suede Shoes (E. Presley); I'm Walkin' (Fats Domino); Blueberry Hill (Fats Domino); Great Balls of Fire (J. Lee Lewis)

The Beatles Vol.3   MMO CDG 1138
Got to Get You into My Life; Lady Madonna; Do You Want to Know a Secret; You've Got to Hide Your Love Away; All You Need is Love; While My Guitar Gently Weeps; Something; Across the Universe ; Drive My Car; Long & Winding Road

MUSIC MINUS ONE COUNTRY

COUNTRY

MALE

Country Male Hits   MMO CDG 103
American Honky-Tonk Bar Association (Garth Brooks);
I'll Leave this World Loving You (Ricky Van Shelton);
T-R-O-U-B-L-E (Travis Tritt); All My Exes Live in Texas
(George Strait); Here's a Quarter (Travis Tritt); Hard Workin'
Man (Brooks & Dunn); Can I Trust You with My Heart (Travis
Tritt); Queen of My Double Wide Trailer (Sammy Kershaw)

Country Male Classics   MMO CDG 104
Always on My Mind (Willie Nelson); Ain't It Funny How Time
Slips Away (Willie Nelson); It's Only Make Believe
(Conway Twitty); I Love a Rainy Night (Eddie Rabbitt);
There's a Fire in the Night (Alabama); What's He Doing in
My World (Eddy Arnold); Guitars, Cadilacs (Dwight Yoakam);
Hello Darlin' (Conway Twitty)

Country Male   MMO CDG 134
What the Cowgirls Do (Vince Gill); Summertime Blues
(Alan Jackson); I Swear (John Michael Montgomery); Little
Less Talk; (Toby Keith); I Cross My Heart (George Strait);
We ShallBe Free (Garth Brooks); She's Not Cryin' Anymore
(Billy Ray Cyrus); Prop Me up Beside the Juke Box
(Joe Diffie)

Hits of Garth Brooks   MMO CDG 1053
Not Counting You; The Dance; Friends in Low Places; Much
Too Young (To Feel this Damned Old); If Tomorrow Never
Comes; Unanswered Prayers; Shameless; Rodeo; The
Thunder Rolls; Two of a Kind, Workin' on a Full House

Hits of Harry Connick, Jr.   MMO CDG 1055
It Had to be You; Our Love is Here to Stay; But Not for Me;
Don't Get Around Much Anymore; Let's Call the Whole
Thing Off; We are in Love; Forever, for Now; Recipe for
Love; It's All Right with Me; I Could Write a Book

Country Men '96   MMO CDG 1212
The Keeper of the Stars; Baby Likes to Rock It;
Pickup Man; This is Me; Storm in the Heartland; You Better
Think Twice; The Fever; Refried Dreams; Stay Forever;
I Should Have Been True

Neil Diamond, Tennesse Moon
MMO CDG 1223
Marry Me; Tennessee Moon; One Good Love; Talking
Optimist Blues; Kentucky Woman; No Limit; Can
Anybody Hear Me; Deep Inside of You; Blue Highway;
A Matter of Love

The Wild West–Garth Brooks   MMO CD 1208
Cowboys and Angels; Rollin'; The Beaches of Cheyenne;
It's Midnight Cinderella; Ireland; The Old Stuff; The Fever;
She's Every Woman; That Ol' Wind; The Change

FEMALE

Hits of Patsy Cline   MMO CDG 101
I Fall to Pieces; Half as Much; Imagine That; Crazy; Three
Cigarettes in an Ashtray; Sweet Dreams; Walkin' After
Midnight; She's Got You

Country Female Hits   MMO CDG 102
Take it Back (Reba McEntire); She's in Love with the Boy
(Trish Yearwood); Down at the Twist and Shout;
(Mary C. Carpenter); Help Me Make it Through the Night
(Sammi Smith); Grandpa (The Judds); Men (Forester
Sisters); Let That Pony Run (Pam Tillis); Stand by Your Man
(Tammy Wynette)

Country Females   MMO CDG 135
XXX'S and OOO'S (Trisha Yearwood); Girls with Guitars
(Wynonna); Piece of My Heart (Faith Hill); He Thinks He'll
Keep Her (Mary Chapin Carpenter); Watch Me (Lorrie
Morgan); Listen to the Radio (Kathy Mattea);
Some Kind of Trouble (Tanya Tucker) • Take it Like a Man
(Michelle Wright)

The Hits of Dolly Parton   MMO CDG 140
Romeo; Yellow Roses; Nine to Five; Jolene; I Will Always
Love You; Hard Candy Christmas; Eagle When She Flies;
Coat of Many Colors

Patsy Cline Hits   MMO CDG 1009
Back in Baby's Arms; Half as Much; San Antonio Rose;
Foolin' Round; Blue Moon of Kentucky; Crazy; She's Got
You; I Fall to Pieces; Sweet Dreams; Walkin' After Midnight

Hits of the Judds   MMO CDG 1033
Maybe Your Baby's Got the Blues; Why Not Me?; Mama
He's Crazy; Have Mercy; Grandpa; A Girl's Night Out;
Change of Heart; Love is Alive; Rockin' With the
Rhythm of the Rain; Give a Little Love

Hits of Reba McEntire   MMO CDG 1034
One Promise Too Late; Whoever's in New England;
Somebody Should Leave; Little Rock; Have I Got a Deal f
or You; What Am I Gonna Do About You; The Last One
to Know; Can't Even Get the Blues; Sunday Kind of Love;
I Know How He Feels

Country Females '96   MMO CDG 1213
I Take My Changes; Whose Bed Have Your Boots Been
Under; Find Out What's Been Happenin'; Cry Wolf;
Independence Day; Wild Love; She Thinks His Name
was John; I Try to Think About Elvis; Heart Over Mind;
When You Walk in the Room

"I have over 100 of your recordings and find them the best for use as background music"

Ruth W
New York, NY

29

Pop songs

Old Time Songs

World's Greatest Sing-Alongs MMO CDG 119
That Old Gang of Mine; Melancholy Baby; Peg O' My Heart; Hail, Hail the Gang's all Here; Alabama Jubilee; Baby Face; I Want to be Happy • Bye Bye Blackbird; Me and My Shadow; Moonlight and Roses; You Were Meant for Me; You are My Sunshine

Old Tyme Sing-Alongs MMO CDG 124
Somebody Stole My Gal; Yes Sir, That's My Baby; Oh, You Beautiful Doll; The Band Played On; The Side-Walks of New York; Take Me Out to the Ball Game; In a Shanty in Old Shanty Town; Heart of My Heart; Alexander's RagTime Band; Margie; Ma, He's Makin' Eyes at Me; Put Your Arms Around Me, Honey; When You Wore a Tulip; Put on Your Old Grey Bonnet; Bill Bailey, Won't You Please Come Home

Happy Songs are Here Again MMO CDG 126
Happy Days are Here Again; I'm Sitting on Top of the World; I'm Looking Over a Four Leaf Clover; My Blue Heaven; Side by Side; When the Red, Red, Robin Comes Bob Bob Bobbin' Along; On The Sunny Side of the Street; Pennies from Heaven; Sweet Georgia Brown; Chicago (That Toddling Town); Forty-Second Street; Lullaby of Broadway; Five Foot Two; Ain't She Sweet; When You're Smiling (The Whole World Smiles with You)

International

Irish Favorites MMO CDG 1210
My Wild Irish Rose; Galway Bay; I'll Take You Home Again Kathleen; Cockles and Mussels; The Isle of Innisfree; The Minstrel Boy; Danny Boy; McNamara's Band; Did Your Mother Come from Ireland?; Dear Old Donegal; The Rose of Tralee; Who Threw the Overalls in Mrs. Murphey's Chowder; When Irish Eyes are Smiling; Whiskey in the Jar; The Gypsy Rover; The Mountains of Mourne; The Wild Rover; A Little Bit of Heaven; Molly Malone; Too-Ra-Loo-Ra-Loo Ra (That's an Irish Lullaby); The Black Velvet Band; The Spinning Wheel; The Wild Colonial Boy

Holidays/Children

Children's Favorites MMO CDG 111
B-I-N-G-O; Are You Sleeping (Freres Jacques); She'll be Comin' 'Round the Mountain; The Muffin Man; The Farmer in the Dell; Reuben, Reuben; Skip to My Lou; London Bridge is Falling Down; Three Blind Mice; Oh! Susannah; Row, Row, Row Your Boat; This Old Man; Lightly Row; Itsy Bitsy Spider; Old MacDonald

Christmas Favorites MMO CDG 112
Deck the Halls • Have Yourself a Merry Little Christmas; We Wish You a Merry Christmas; We Three Kings of Orient Are; It Came Upon a Midnight Clear; Jingle Bells; Hark! The Herald Angels Sing; Silent Night

Christmas Memories MMO CDG 1203
Joy to the World; It Came upon a Midnight Clear; O Come, O Come, Emmanuel; Hark! The Herald Angels Sing; O Holy Night; O Come All Ye Faithful; O Little Town of Bethlehem; Silent Night; The Twelve Days of Christmas; Jingle Bells; Auld Lang Syne

Special Occasions

Songs for a Wedding Vol. 1 MMO CDG 1083
There is Love; And I Love You So; Through the Eyes of Love; One Hand, One Heart; Longer; Wedding March (Recessional); You're My Everything; Through the Years; Don't Know Much; Somewhere Out There; Up Where We Belong

Songs for a Wedding Vol. 2 MMO CDG 1084
Somewhere; Daddy's Little Girl; We've Only Just Begun; Could I Have this Dance?; The Greatest Love of All; On the Wings of Love; You Take My Breath Away; The Rose; Always; The Wind Beneath My Wings

True Companion-Love Songs for a Wedding MMO CDG 128
Inseperable (Natalie Cole); You and I (E. Rabbitt & C. Gayle); I Will Always Love You (Whitney Houston); All I Have (Beth Nielsen Chapman); Beautiful in My Eyes (Joshua Kadison); True Companion (Marc Cohn); When You Tell Me (J. Iglesias/D. Parton); The Man in Love with You (George Strait)

Broadway and FILM

A unique collection of accompanient recordings covering all the great works of Musical Theatre. Printed lyrics included. Part of MMO's library of over 10,000 popular songs. Complete and accompaniment versions of each show, including overtures are offered. Among our most popular offerings.

Les Misérables/Phantom of the Opera MMO CD 1016/PS 419/420
Boublii/Schonberg: I Dreamed A Dream; Castle on a Cloud; Stars; On My Own;Bring Him Home; Think of Me
Lloyd-Webber: Phantom of the Opera;The Music of the Night; All I Ask of You; Wishing You Were Somehow Here Again

Guys And Dolls MMO CD 1067/PS 419/420
Loesser: Fugue for Tinhorns; I'll Know; A Bushel and a Peck; Adelaide's Lament; Guys And Dolls; If I Were a Bell; I've Never Been in Love Before; Take Back Your Mink; More I Cannot Wish You Luck be a Lady; Sue Me; Sit Down You're Rockin' The Boat; Marry the Man Today

West Side Story (2 CD set) MMO CD 1100/PS 419/420
Bernstein: Prologue; Jet Song; Something's Coming; The Dance At The Gym; Maria; Tonight; America; Cool; One Hand, One Heart; Tonight (Balcony Scene); The Rumble; I Feel Pretty; Somewhere; Gee, Officer Krupke!; A Boy Like That

Cabaret (2 CD set) MMO CD 1110/PS 419/420
Ebb/Kander: Willkommen; Mein Herr; Don't Tell Mamma; Maybe this Time; Perfectly Marvelous; Two Ladies; it Couldn't Please Me More; Tommorow Belongs to Me; Why Shouldn't I Wake Up; The Money Song - Sitting Pretty; If You Could See Her; Cabaret

MUSIC MINUS ONE SHOWS

South Pacific   MMO CD 1177/PS 419/420
Rodgers & Hammerstein, Jr: Overture; Dites - Moi; A Cock-Eyed Optimist; Twin Soliloquies; Some Enchanted Evening; Bloody Mary; There is Nothin' Like a Dame; Bali Ha'i; I'm Gonna Wash that Man Right Out-a My Hair; A Wonderful Guy; Younger than Springtime; Happy Talk; Honey Bun; You've Got to be Carefully Taught; This Nearly was Mine

The King and I (2 CD set)
MMO CD1178/PS419/420
Rodgers & Hammerstein, Jr: I Whistle a Happy Tune; My Lord and Master; Hello Young Lovers; A Puzzlement; Getting to Know You; We Kiss in a Shadow; Shall I Tell You What I Think of You; Something Wonderful; I Have Dreamed; Shall We Dance;

Fiddler on the Roof
MMO CD 1179/PS 419/420
Harnick & Bock: Tradition; Matchmaker, Matchmaker; If I Were a Rich Man; Sabbath Prayer; To Life (La Chaim); Miracle of Miracles; Tevye's Dream; Sunrise Sunset; Now I Have Everthing; Do You Love Me?; Far from the Home I Love; Anatevka

Carousel   MMO CD 1180/PS 419/420
Rodgers & Hammerstein, Jr: The Carousel Waltz; You're a Queer One, Julie Jordon; Mister Snow; If I Loved You; June is Bustin' Out All Over; When the Children are Asleep; Blow Low, Blow High; Soliloquy (My Boy Bill); A Real Nice Clambake; Stonecutters Cut it on Stone; What's the Use of Wonderin'; You'll Never Walk Alone; The Highest Judge of All

Porgy And Bess   MMO CD 1181/PS 419/420
Gershwin & Gershwin: Summertime; A Woman is a Sometime Thing; Gone, Gone, Gone; My Man's Gone Now; I Got Plenty O' Nuttin'; Bess, You is My Woman Now; Oh I Can't Sit Down; It Ain't Necessarily So; Starwberry Woman; I Loves You Porgy; Oh, Heav'nly Father; There's a Boat Dat's Leavin' Soon for NY; Bess, Oh Where's My Bess?; Oh Lawd, I'm on My Way

The Music Man   MMO CD 1183/PS 419/420
Willson: Overture; Iowa Stubborn; Ya Got Trouble; If You Don't Mind My Saying So; Goodnight My Someone; Seventy-Six Trombones; Sincere The Sadder but Wiser Girl; Pick a Little/Talk a Little; Goodnight Ladies; Marian the Librarian; My White Knight; The Wells Fargo Wagon; Shipoop; Lida Rose/Will I Ever Tell You; Gary Indiana; Till There was You; Interlude

Showboat   MMO CD 1184/PS 419/420
Kern: Opening: Cotton Blossom; Make Believe; Ol' Man River; Can't Help Lovin' Dat Man of Mine; Life Upon the Wicked Stage; Till Good Luck Comes My Way; I Might Fall Back on You; You Are Love; Why Do I Love You; Bill; After The Ball

Annie Get Your Gun (2 CD set)
MMO CD 1186/PS 419/420
Berlin: Overture; Colonel Buffalo Bill; I'm a Bad,Bad Man; Doin' What Comes Naturally; The Girl that I Marry; You Can't Get a Man With a Gun; There's No Business like Show Business; They Say it's Wonderful; Moonshine Lullaby; There's No Business like Show Business (Reprise); My Defenses are Down; I'm an Indian Too; You Can't Get a Man With a Gun (Reprise); I Got Lost in His Arms; I Got the Sun in the Morning; Old Fashioned Wedding; The Girl that I Marry (Reprise); Anything You Can Do

Hello Dolly (2 CD set)   MMO CD 1187/PS 419/420
Herman: Overture; Opening; Act 1; I Put My Hand In; It Takes a Woman; Put on Your Sunday Clothes; Ribbons Down My Back; Dancing; Before the Parade Passes By; Elegance; Hello Dolly; It Only Takes a Moment; So Long, Dearie; Finale Ultimo

Oliver (2 CD set)   MMO CD 1189/PS 419/420
Bart/Bricusse: Overture; Food, Glorius Food; Oliver; I Shall Scream; Boy for Sale; That's Your Funeral; Where is Love; Consider Yourself; Pick a Pocket or Two; It's a Fine Life; I'd Do Anthing; Be Back Soon; Oom-Pah-Pah; My Name; As Long as He Needs Me; Where is Love(Reprise); Who Will Buy; It's a Fine Life (Reprise); Reviewing the Situation; Oliver (Reprise); Reviewing the Situation (Reprise); Finale

Sunset Boulevard   MMO CD 1193/PS 419/420
Lloyd-Webber: Surrender; With One Look; The Greatest Star of All; Girl Meets Boy; New Ways to Dream; The Perfect Year; Sunset Boulevard; As if We Never Said Goodbye; Too Much in Love to Care

Grease   MMO CD 1196/PS1505
Summer Nights; Rock 'N'Roll is Here to Stay; Sandy; Hopelessly Devoted to You; You're the One that I Want: Grease; Greased Lightnin; Born to Hand Jive; We Go Together; Look at Me, I'm Sandra Dee; Those Magic Changes; There are Worse Things That I Could Do; Blue Moon

Smokey Joe's Cafe   MMO CD 1197/PS 2340
On Broadway; Poison Ivy; Charlie Brown; Stand by Me; Loving You; Hound Dog; There Goes My Baby; Jailhouse Rock; Spanish Harlem; Yakety Yak

> *"Cabaret was our school musical this year and your CD sounds just like the pit orchestra in performance. Congratulations on a job well done!"*
>
> Donald D.
> Illinois

Walt Disney Favorite Songs   MMO CD 1198
Can You Feel the Love Tonight: Circle of Love, Hakuna Matata, The Lion Sleeps Tonight; Colors of the Wind; If I Never Knew You: Just Around the River Bend: Be Our Guest: Beauty and the Beast: A Whole New World: Under the Sea.

Waiting to Exhale, Vol.1
MMO CDG 1206/PSCDG1206
Exhale (Whitney Houston); Let It Flow (Toni Braxton); My Funny Valentine (Chaka Khan); My Love, My Sweet Love (Patti Labelle); Why Does It Hurt So Bad? (Whitney Houston); It Hurts Like Hell (Aretha Franklin); Count on Me (Whitney Houston/Cece Winans) ; Sittin' Up in My Room (Brandy)

Waiting to Exhale, Vol.
MMO CDG 1207/PS CDG 1207
This is How It Works (TLC); All Night Long (SWV); Kissing You (Faith Evans) ; And I Give My Love to You (Sonja Marie); Not Gon' Cry (Mary J. Blige); How Could You Call Her Baby? (Shanna); Love Will Be Waiting at Home (For Real)

Mr. Holland's Opus   MMO CDG 1209/PS CDG1209
Visions of a Sunset (Shawn Stockman); One, Two, Three (Len Barry) ; Uptight-Everything's Alright (Stevie Wonder); A Lover's Concerto (The Toys); Imagine (John Lennon); Beautiful Boy-Darling Boy (John Lennon/Yoko Ono); The Pretender (Jackson Browne); Cole's Song (Julian Lennon); I've Got a Woman (Ray Charles); Someone to Watch Over Me (Julia Fordham)

Miss Saigon   MMO CD 1226
Schonberg/Maltby Jr./Boublil: The Heat is On in Saigon; The Movie in My Mind; Why God Why?; The Last Night of the World; I Still Believe; The American Dream

---

Jekyll & Hyde   MMO CD 1151/PS 419/420
Wildhorn & Bricusse: This is the moment, Love Has Come of Age, Once Upon a Dream, Someone Like You, Till You Came into My Life, No One Knows Who I Am, A New Life, Once Upon

Camelot   MMO CD 1173/PS 419/420
Lerner & Loewe: I Wonder what the King is Doing Tonight; The Simple Joys of Maidenhood; Camelot; Follow Me; C'est Moi; The Lusty Month of May; How to Handle a Woman; Before I Gaze at You Again; If Ever I Would Leave You; What do the Simple Folks Do?; I Loved You Once in Silence

My Fair Lady (2 CD set)   MMO CD 1174/PS 419/420
Lerner & Loewe: Overture;Why Can't the English; Wouldn't It be Loverly; With a Little Bit of Luck; I'm an Ordinary Man; Just You Wait; The Rain in Spain; I Could of Danced All Night; The Ascot Gavotte;On the Street Where You Live; You Did It; Show Me; Get Me to the Church on Time; A Hymn to Him; Without You;I've Grown Accustomed to Her Face

Oklahoma   MMO CD 1175/PS 419/420
Rodgers & Hammerstein, Jr: Oh What a Beautiful Morning; Surry with the Fringe on the Top; Kansas City; I Can't Say No; Many a New Day; People Will Say We're in Love; Por Jud is Daid; Lonely Room; Out of My Dreams; The Farmer and the Cowman; All 'er Nothin';Oklahoma

The Sound Of Music   MMO CD 1176/PS 419/420
Rodgers & Hammerstein, Jr: Overture; The Sound of Music; Maria; My Favorite Things; Do Re Mi; Sixteen Going on Seventeen; The Lonely Goatheard; How Can Love Survive; So Long Farewell; Climb Every Mountain; No Way to Stop It; An Ordinary Couple; Canticle: Confitemini Domine; Edelweiss

Small numbers on far right indicate the cassette edition of each album

All MMO CD's are $22.98 each
including printed music part
2 CD Sets are $29.98 each
4 CD Sets are $49.98 each
7 CD Set (Rutgers Music Dictation Series) is $98.50